CU00970912

Coming Down in the Drink

Coming Down in the Drink

The Survival of Bomber Goldfish, John Brennan DFC

Sean Feast

Pen & Sword
AVIATION

First published in Great Britain in 2017 by
Pen & Sword Aviation
an imprint of
Pen & Sword Books Ltd
47 Church Street
Barnsley
South Yorkshire
S70 2AS

Copyright © Sean Feast 2017

ISBN 978 1 47389 153 1

The right of Sean Feast to be identified as the Author of this Work
has been asserted by him in accordance with the Copyright, Designs
and Patents Act 1988.

A CIP catalogue record for this book is available from the British
Library

All rights reserved. No part of this book may be reproduced or
transmitted in any form or by any means, electronic or mechanical
including photocopying, recording or by any information storage
and retrieval system, without permission from the Publisher in
writing.

Typeset in Ehrhardt by
Mac Style Ltd, Bridlington, East Yorkshire
Printed and bound in the UK by TJ International Ltd. Padstow

Pen & Sword Books Ltd incorporates the imprints of Pen & Sword
Archaeology, Atlas, Aviation, Battleground, Discovery, Family
History, History, Maritime, Military, Naval, Politics, Railways,
Select, Transport, True Crime, Fiction, Frontline Books, Leo
Cooper, Praetorian Press, Seaforth Publishing and Wharncliffe.

For a complete list of Pen & Sword titles please contact
PEN & SWORD BOOKS LIMITED
47 Church Street, Barnsley, South Yorkshire, S70 2AS, England
E-mail: enquiries@pen-and-sword.co.uk
Website: www.pen-and-sword.co.uk

Contents

Acknowledgements

My thanks first and foremost go to John himself, a most distinguished gentleman. It has been an honour and a privilege to be able to tell his story and reminisce on a remarkable wartime career. Since being introduced by Ed Toop, we have spent a most enjoyable twelve months getting John's adventures down on paper. Through the wonders of the 'world wide web', I found Pierre Michiels, a keen aviation enthusiast, who in turn introduced me to Ceanan Baird, son of the late Squadron Leader, The Honourable Robert Baird. Ceanan was extremely helpful in answering my questions and in very kindly allowing me sight of his father's log book and photographs, some of which are reproduced in this book. John's own log book was stolen, and so having access to another contemporary source was most helpful in piecing together John's time in the Middle East. Other thanks go to: Tace Fox, archivist at Harrow School who provided information on Donald Crossley; Art Stacey, Treasurer/Membership Secretary of the Goldfish Club; and Sally Overthrow at the Ministry of Defence Medal Office. My work colleagues Alex, Imogen and Toto always deserve special mention for keeping me sane and allowing me the odd absence without question. Iona will be back soon! And finally to my genius wife Elaine, and two sons Matt and James who I hope never have to face the hardships that John and his contemporaries had to endure.

Chapter 1

The Waiting Game

John Brennan never had to go to war. He certainly didn't have to fight for the British. But somehow it just seemed like the right thing to do at the time.

The interview at the recruitment centre in Acton was the usual perfunctory affair. He'd arrived having sniffed the cold morning air on that January day in 1940 with his mind clear and his urge to 'do his duty' apparent to anyone who might ask him to sign on the dotted line.

The desk sergeant showed no surprise at John's Irish accent. But then why should he? Since the Famine there had been an Exodus of Irishmen to England, to escape starvation and seek salvation elsewhere. Hadn't the waterways and railways that criss-crossed the nation been built with the blood, sweat and cursing of the Irish Navvy? This was not the first, and certainly would not be the last Irishman to want to become a pilot.

The sergeant, John thought, was probably old enough to have been in the first 'show'. The faded medal ribbon on his wingless breast pocket suggested that he had, and perhaps accounted for the warmth with which the young man's zeal to join His Majesty's Royal Air Force was received.

Unusually, John was the only man in the queue and struck something of a forlorn figure. Not usually backward in coming forward, he hesitated slightly before daring to speak, at which point the sergeant looked up and smiled. John recalls:

Some will ask why I, as an Irishman, wanted to fight for the British when it was not my war. That is difficult to explain because whatever it was, it was felt by many thousands like me in the First World War and carried over into the second. It was our country.

'I was the only one volunteering that day, or so it seemed. And I wanted to join the RAF. I'd read in the national newspapers about the exciting trips that the heroic crews of the Wellingtons and Whitleys were flying over Germany, and that on occasion they had to fight off determined attacks from the German Luftwaffe. In the thick of the action were the air gunners, and despite never once having fired a shot in anger or even having held a gun or rifle, I was determined to become one of their number.

To John's surprise, the RAF did not seem in a particular hurry to deploy his services. He was told he would have to be patient, and return at a later date when he would be up before an aircrew selection board to assess his suitability for operational flying. John was happy. He was in no particular rush himself. He had learned to be patient; learned to take disappointment and rejection. He'd worked hard to get where he was, and another few weeks was not going to make any difference. Besides, he had a girlfriend to keep him company that he hoped he would one day marry. So he could wait.

*   *   *

John Michael Brennan was born on 5 January 1921 in Ballylinan, a small, farming village in the parish of Castlecomer, County Kilkenny. His father had been in the 1st Battalion of the Royal Dublin Fusiliers and fought with the British Army in Gallipoli. His battalion suffered heavy casualties and was for a short time merged with another unit, the 1 Royal Munster Fusiliers to become 'The Dubsters'. He was eventually evacuated in January 1916.

Returning to Ireland after the war, John's father worked briefly in the local coalmines until the coming of the Irish Free State in 1922 when he joined the newly formed Irish Army and was posted to Callins Barracks, Cork, where he served until retirement. An intelligent and capable man, he was offered a commission but turned it down, preferring to stay among the ranks as a non-commissioned officer.

John lived with his parents at Evergreen Road (in the south of the City) for six years. The house was particularly small and the rooms sparse, with little by way of any mod cons or even furniture. There was a main room with a coal fire where they did the cooking and huddled for warmth, and a slightly larger room that was divided by curtains into bedrooms. There was nothing 'cosy' about it; it was, in fact, thoroughly miserable.

Whereas some small boys can escape the misery of home and find refuge at school, for John there was no respite. The North Monastery School, to the north beyond the River Lee, was part of a much larger building and the windows were covered with a wire mesh that allowed layers of rubbish and detritus to congregate. It was a thoroughly depressing place, dank and dark, like something one would imagine in a Dickens novel rather than twentieth century Ireland. The head teacher was a priest, and the staff comprised both priests, monks and lay teachers.

When I was at the North Monastery School, each day at about midday a monk would enter the classroom. He must have been in his eighties. He would instruct us to go to our catechisms and study a certain chapter. He would then sit in a chair and bring out a small metal case that he would open with his thumb and forefinger, bring out a pinch of snuff, and inhale. After a few

moments we were subjected to a fit of coughing and sneezing,
after which he would pull at a large cloth which had started out
white and was now covered in ugly brown stains. When he had
finished, his eyes bulged like those of a seal.

John was a journeyman schoolboy who found solace in long distance
running and English composition:

I was very keen on the English language, and used to write stories.
Every Christmas there was a competition in the school for the
best composition – and the year before I left, the teacher tasked
with judging the competition was a Lieutenant in the IRA who
had been involved in the 1916 rising and had stopped a bullet in
the knee. He walked with a permanent limp.

We were given subjects to write about and one was Irish
history – so I thought I would create a story about the Easter
Rising. It was full of descriptive nouns and hyperbole, building
an image of a desperate action, the storming of the post office and
the heroic patriots fighting to the last drop of blood and refusing
to surrender. Perhaps not surprisingly it appealed to the judge
and I won first prize. Knowing how religious my mother was,
I chose as my prize a large portrait of Christ, thinking that she
would like it, and like me. But I was wrong.

John's mother and father had seven children in all. John had an
older sister, Maureen, who died young of meningitis. After John
there was Elizabeth (known as Katherine b.1923); Pauline (b.1925);
Alice (b.1927); a brother Michael (b.1929); and another sister Phylis
(b.1935). Accommodation became so crowded that John used to hang
his clothes on what he called 'Paddy's nail' – that is to say the floor!
John's memories and impressions of those early days are stark:

Ireland in the 1920s and 1930s reminded me very much of what it must have been like living in a communist country, where instead of an all-powerful state we were ruled by an all-powerful church. There was nothing benevolent about it; it could be intimidating and markedly hierarchical: the priests were the saints; we people were the sinners. It was black and white. They seemed to have everything and we appeared to have nothing, and that was how it was meant to be.

The priests would come around regularly to our houses and walk in without being invited. They would question us about our attendance at Mass, and chastise us for not putting sufficient funds into the collection. They had total control, and it's not an exaggeration to say that many of us were afraid of them.

In c1928, when I was about seven, we moved to the north of the City but only stayed a short while before moving out into the country, about two miles from Blarney. My father, who was still in the army, would cycle to the barracks every morning and if I was lucky he would give me a lift on his handlebars. It was not the most comfortable journey into school but it was still better than walking.

Living in the country, and close to a farm, had its advantages. At home, his main meal comprised a stew, and never without a packet of Edwards desiccated soup. From the farm, John could enjoy a breakfast of bacon and eggs:

The farm was owned by an elderly lady whose husband had died. She welcomed an extra pair of hands around the place and to do the shopping, and so I would help out most weekends and during the holidays and be paid 50p a week for my troubles. I thought I was rich.

I also ate like a prince. Dinner was often a joint of boiled beef with vegetables, and potatoes boiled in their jackets. After being strained, they were tipped out on the middle of the table and onto a newspaper that served as a tablecloth. In the corner of the kitchen was a small churn of buttermilk and we would help ourselves.

There was another farm that delivered milk, daily, to the city (I learned metal measurements in pints and half pint). Again, if I was lucky, I could hitch a lift on the cart and the farmer would take me into town. The only drawback to this otherwise splendid arrangement was that the mule that pulled the cart would let rip with a disgusting smell from its bottom in rhythm with its walk, and I was sat right behind it!

Being catholic, religion played a significant part in his early life.

Every night at about 9.00pm we had to go down on our knees for the evening prayers. My father would have his rosary beads and as he recited the 'Hail Mary's' and the Lord's Prayer we had to repeat after him.

One of my father's friends won £10,000 in the Irish Sweepstake and some time afterwards we were invited to tea in their new home. There were all sorts of sandwiches and cakes and it was fabulous. Thereafter we were told to pray to the Virgin Mary every night so that we would win the sweepstake too. I don't think I prayed hard enough.

John was also obliged to attend Mass each Sunday, and that meant getting up at 6.30 in the morning to walk to the church in Blarney in time for the 8.00am service.

We could never be late. Halfway along the dirt road was a thick, wooded area with dense undergrowth. My mother, who suffered with chronic constipation, would regularly nip into the woods and tell me to keep watch and call out if someone was coming. They never did.

Until now I have not said much about my mother. The truth is, I never liked her and she never liked me. Indeed I don't think she ever liked any of us. She certainly didn't love us. I never once saw her cuddle or show any sign of affection to any of her children. She was a cold, unloving and unlovely woman with sharp features and glasses who never smiled, never laughed, and never had a good word to say about anyone. She never had any friends, and I never saw her make friends or even have a friendly conversation. She was, frankly, odd. I am not even convinced that she had her faith.

My mother took a particular dislike to my sister Alice, though why I cannot say, but at one time she went to live with my grandmother. One day Alice was out playing, fell over badly and fractured her nose. It was never attended to properly, and my mother would taunt her by calling her 'pug nose'. Alice died a few years later of TB.

The family moved back into the city when John was about 11 and lived in a flat above a public house close to the barrack gates. If he looked hard enough through the grimy windows, he could just make out the barrack clock, and used that as his guide for getting to school on time. They were not there for long before being obliged to move on again when the lease came to an end and so found new accommodation some 200 yds away in another flat above yet another pub. It was managed by Mrs Shannon, a widow whose kindliness was not reciprocated by John's mother:

Each week Mrs Shannon would climb up the ladder to clean the windows and my mother would remark: 'There she goes again, showing us her drawers.' On reflection it may sound funny, but there was never any amusement in her voice.

While living above the pub, John was hauled out of his bed one night and told to get dressed. He was then frogmarched by his mother to their old stamping ground in Evergreen Road, about three miles away.

A family of three brothers lived there who were about the same age as my father. When we arrived at their house, my mother knocked forcefully on their front door and waited. Finally it was opened by one of the brothers and my mother stepped inside to see my father, sat at the table, playing cards. She looked at him, turned on her heels and marched out again. It was only when I was getting undressed much later that a realised my boots were on the wrong feet.

John's mother also took a dislike to another neighbour:

They had only recently moved in and were Scottish, and had two teenage girls. My mother forbade me to have anything to do with them because they were Protestants.

The mood in our house was determined by my mother's frame of mind. My father would come home at the same time every evening, take off his jacket and boots, and never speak a word. There was nearly always a sinister and unsettling atmosphere, like we were expecting something to happen, but couldn't predict what or when. She would give him his supper but almost begrudged having to feed us children. She could also be cruel.

My school was more than a mile from our new home, a long walk for a small boy with a school bag but even longer with an armful of heavy shopping on the way home. My mother would oblige me to wait in the morning for her shopping list, but not give me the list until she knew it would make me late for school which meant a beating. If I dared to try and hurry her up, she would sneer: 'You wait 'til I'm ready', and make me wait even longer. My tardiness would inevitably make trouble for me at school, and I became quite adept at making excuses.

On another occasion, she told me to go into town to buy some syrup of figs. She put 2/6 (about twelve and a half pence) into a piece of paper and warned me not to lose it. I ran down to the chemists, but when I got there the money had gone. My heart sank to my boots as I wondered what to do. I decided to retrace my steps, slowly, in the hope of finding it, my eyes glued to the ground. It wasn't until I was three quarters of the way home that I spotted the money on the road, still wrapped in its paper. Of course when I finally got home I was chastised for taking so long.

One afternoon, sometime later, I was again sent out on an errand into town and told to hurry so I ran. Unfortunately I tripped, fell heavily and grazed my knee. When I got home, my father put a dirty rag on it. The pain was such that I couldn't sleep and in the morning my knee had swollen badly and there was a large lump under my left arm. I was taken down to the barracks to see the MO. He pulled the rag from my wound, causing me much distress, and put a clean dressing on it that had to be reapplied each week for the next month. Even after it finally healed, infected spots would appear every so often.

While his mother showed no maternal instincts, others were more kind.

We bought bread at a bakery in the far south of the city, a long way from our flat, but owned and managed by a distant relative who looked like Lord Kitchener with the most improbable comedic moustaches. His sister worked with him in the shop and used to take pity on my puny frame, and feed me up with a freshly buttered roll that tasted simply heavenly.

I also remember a grocery shop that sold salted, dried cod. As a child the fillets looked like bats hanging from the ceiling. After soaking the fish overnight, we would eat some, every Friday with mashed potatoes. It was one of the few fond memories I have of my childhood.

*   *   *

As a teenager John began, as most teenagers do, to become more aware about his body and appearance. He wanted to look smarter, and began applying Brylcreem in his hair. He suffered while his mother continued to berate him until at last, at 16 years of age, he was old enough to escape. From his wages helping on the farm, and picking up odd jobs, he had saved sufficient money to afford a crossing:

I spent some days studying the timetable of the Ferries that sailed from Cork Quay and saving enough money to make it to London. I left the house at 5.00pm in the early evening, with no possessions other than the Confirmation suit I was wearing, and made my way first to retrieve the savings that I had hidden behind a loose stone in a wall at the back of the flat where we had once lived.

I strolled down to the quay; it was a comparatively mild evening for the time of year (January, 1937) and the Irish Sea appeared very calm. I had already purchased my ticket and boarded the ferry without fuss, and made my way to the upper deck. I sat on that deck all night, staring out to sea and thinking about the adventure that lay ahead. As we approached the Welsh coast, I could see the twinkling lights and fires of the steel mills that became more vibrant as we approached.

Upon disembarking, John followed a number of passengers snaking their way slowly to the railway station. Many were young, like him, leaving behind past lives and looking to the future with renewed hope. Some were older, perhaps joining those who had already arrived and made their mark. All were looking for a better life.

John boarded the train that went to Paddington, a destination that, until then, meant little or nothing to the young traveller. But his was a well-trodden path. On the grubby platform, as though expecting him, was a small group of older men and women in an incongruous dark blue uniform and red tabs that he recognised as that of The Salvation Army, that magnificent organisation that since the 1860s had rendered such important service to the poor, the hungry, the homeless and the destitute. John was far from destitute, neither was he especially poor – not with his £4.50 in savings burning a hole in his suit pocket. But he was hungry, and certainly in need of a bed for the night.

He was given the address of a Salvation Army hostel in the Marylebone Road where he could stay for sixpence a night. It was a pleasant enough place; clean, if not especially warm. He slept sufficiently well and in the morning set out to find a job. From the Marylebone Road he walked along the Edgware Road and into Hyde Park. It was raining hard, but John appeared not to notice. London seemed a marvellous city, full of new sights and sounds. Filled with hope, he saw his first set of traffic lights and marvelled at how the green, amber and red colours reflected on the wet roads.

He continued walking along Oxford Street until he came to the Cumbernauld Hotel where he had heard that he might find work:

I went around the back where the kitchens were and enquired whether there were any jobs going. I had my school-leaving certificate with me as the only evidence of any qualifications and the man took it from me and went inside. He returned shortly after to tell me that, unfortunately, there was nothing for me but that he had heard that the ABC chain of restaurants in Oxford Street was taking people in. I thanked him and left. I never did get my certificate back!

John had better luck at the ABC. He was interviewed and given a job as a kitchen porter for which he would receive 18/6 per week, working 7.00am to 5.00pm Monday to Friday and from 7.00am to 12 noon on Saturdays. He was told to report to the ABC's Victoria restaurant:

The restaurant was notable for having enormous mirrors on every wall and my first job was to clean them. It took most of the day and by the end of it I was exhausted.

ABC was one of the big food success stories of the nineteenth and twentieth century. Developed out of the Aerated Bread Company, at its peak in 1923 it had 150 branch shops in London and 250 tea shops, second only to the slightly more famous Lyons corner houses.

Life in the kitchens was hard. There was little or nothing by way of modern appliances or equipment, and cleaning the seemingly endless supply of pots and pans with small amounts of soap and large amounts of effort and elbow grease was a thankless and tiring job. But it had its advantages. John was fed well – and particularly looked forward to fish and chips with large dollops of tomato ketchup on a Friday – and began to learn other skills from those around him. He watched the pastry chef, especially, and the chef was kind enough to teach John something of the art. John learned sufficient that when the pastry chef left, he was asked whether he could take on the task. He seized the opportunity, creating all manner of fruit pies, sponges and ice cream to satisfy the needs of London's hungry workers. John worked well and he worked hard, seeing his salary more than double.

John's change in fortunes allowed him to move out of the hostel and into digs. He had even more money when he was promoted to second chef:

> *I heard that there were some rooms to rent in Chippenham Road and when I got there I found the front door was ajar. I pushed it open to see the landlady waiting at the top of the stairs. She welcomed me in and asked me my name to which I replied 'Brennan' and thereafter that's what she called me!*

John had landed on his feet. The Roberts family were most hospitable: Mr Roberts was Irish and had two sons of similar age to John. Mrs Roberts was caring but not intrusive, and he became part of the family:

> *At the restaurant we would eat twice, with a hearty breakfast in the morning and lunch at around 2.30 after all of the diners had gone. Because I did not have much money to spare, I rarely ate in the evenings and I think Mrs Roberts noticed. One Sunday I was asked if I'd like to sit with them for supper which comprised the most delicious roast lamb, roast potatoes, greens and mint sauce, followed by apple pie. I thought I'd died and gone to heaven. We talked a great deal but she never once questioned me about my family or why I had left Ireland. She was very discrete.*
>
> *Mrs Roberts belonged to a savings club, to which she contributed half a crown a week and in return could buy all manner of items. Kind lady that she was she ordered me a new suit, shirts, socks, and underwear such that I was probably the best-dressed second*

chef in the country. I bought myself a silk handkerchief for my
pocket and looked a proper dandy about town.

John had been working in London for almost a year when the grapevine
started humming again, and he heard that the Great Western Railway
(GWR) was recruiting chefs. GWR, sometimes referred to as 'God's
Wonderful Railway' by its supporters, had only recently celebrated
its centenary and had invested in new carriages and rolling stock.
Although the firm had struggled during the depression, it was
mounting something of a comeback, and was still popular with those
seeking a holiday on the beaches of Devon and Cornwall.

The ABC restaurants had been good to him, but he had more than
repaid them the opportunity with hard work, and decided the railways
held the promise of a little adventure:

> *I was interviewed by the catering manager and started work*
> *the next day. I was put on a train to Minehead, and visited all*
> *of the top tourist destinations of the time including Newquay,*
> *Penzance, Plymouth etc.*
>
> *The galley in which we had to prepare food for the travelling*
> *public was very small which made our life incredibly difficult. It*
> *was made more difficult still by my fellow chef who was huge!*
> *By the end of my time with GWR, I too was a little larger as we*
> *were especially well fed and any tips that we received as a team*
> *were shared out evenly so I had more money in my pocket.*

Throughout the summer season, factories in London and the Midlands
with social clubs would arrange excursions for their staff to visit resorts
on the western coast. Trains could be full with up to 200 or so workers,
and John was part of the team responsible for providing their lunch on
the outward journey and tea on their return.

GWR was impressed with their young Irish chef, so much so that at the end of the season they offered him a permanent role. Unfortunately, John was obliged to decline, on account of not being able to produce a birth certificate. This minor setback did not last long, however, and soon after John applied for and secured a role at the Walls Ice Cream factory in Acton. It was not long before he got chatting to an attractive young machine operator named Angela, and treated her to a night out at the cinema to watch the latest Laurel and Hardy, *Chumps at Oxford*.

> *I only left GWR because I didn't have a birth certificate. If I had known then what I know now, that I could have obtained a copy from Somerset House for 2/6, I would have stayed, which meant I would never have gone to work for Walls, never have met Angela, and wouldn't have the family that I have today.*

*   *   *

The tranquil summer of 1939 soon gave way to the brooding storm clouds of war. Many had seen it coming. John had followed the rise of Hitler in the newspapers and on the newsreels; he had read about the Fuhrer's occupation of the Sudetenland and march into Austria, and Britain's paltry response. Now it was the turn of Poland, and the declaration of war. By the summer of 1940, John was a proud member of the Royal Air Force Volunteer Reserve (RAFVR). His long wait to join the fight ended on 4 July, when he was at last instructed to proceed to RAF Uxbridge to be processed as 'aircrew under training':

> *At the selection board I had said that I wanted to be an air gunner, but the wise men behind the desk put me forward as a wireless op/air gunner, even though I had no interest in or pre-disposition towards radio, or even electronics for that matter.*

They asked me various questions about my attitude towards discipline and my impression on the war. It felt like more of a social conversation than an interview. Then I was given a medical of which I remember little other than being told to blow a small ball up a tube and hold it there for a minute while they tested the strength in my lungs. They also tested my eyes and probed around in my ears to ensure I was neither colour blind nor deaf.

The last test involved me being placed in a swivel chair and spun around by the MO who then took my blood pressure. I assume it was to test my resistance to air sickness, but whatever it was I passed!

At Uxbridge, John was kitted out in serge blue, given a railway warrant and instructed to report to the Initial Training Wing (ITW) in Blackpool, the rite of passage for every RAF fledgling. He was billeted in what passed for a boarding house that, in the height of summer, had no doubt entertained hundreds of families seeking holiday fun at the beach. There was not that much fun to be had now:

There were five of us accommodated in each house where we slept and were fed, although food seemed to be rationed. Our landlady used to put the butter on one side of the knife to spread it and then take it off with the other!

At ITW, John was introduced to the rudiments of air force life, with hours of classroom instruction punctuated by commensurate hours in intensely monotonous square bashing and drill. They were accompanied at all times by the archetypal RAF corporal, who had slogged for over a decade to attain his rank and appeared to despise wholeheartedly these airmen who might achieve superior rank in months rather than years.

*We had the obligatory corporal who would shout at us all the time
and question our parentage but having been used to home, and the
attitude of my mother, I took it all in my stride. Some silly sods
would call me 'spud' or 'paddy' but I just laughed it off. I just
saw it as a process, a means to an end, and was happy that my
training was at last underway.*

After ITW there was a pause in John's progress. The RAF was at that
stage still learning how to cope with the hundreds of young men who
had volunteered for aircrew, and the infrastructure was not yet fully in
place to cope with the numbers. Later, in 1943-44, training ran like a
well-oiled machine at the peak of performance, whereas in 1940 there
was a will, but not always the way.

John was posted to RAF Binbrook in Lincolnshire, a new airfield that
was still in the process of being built. Diggers and other mechanical
machinery lay all around, and Binbrook did not yet have the air or the
appearance of a fully operational base. Despite having no knowledge
of weaponry beyond a Lee Enfield rifle, John was allocated to ground
defence duties and put in charge of a 20mm canon, sited on the airfield
perimeter:

*There were two of us on duty 24 hours on/off and we would
take it in turns to man the gun. We were in a gun pit that offered
some shelter, although we kept a brazier burning throughout the
day and night to keep warm. There were, I believe, about three
such anti-aircraft gun emplacements to protect against enemy
intruders.*

Although towards the north of the country, the airfield was not immune
from enemy attack.

The Battle of Britain was in full swing and we read about our heroic Spitfire and Hurricane pilots shooting down the Luftwaffe. Then one day the battle came to us. The siren sounded and we could hear and then see in the distance what I took to be a Dornier 217[1] approaching.

The bomber was definitely making an attack and as it got closer I could clearly see it open its bomb doors and almost immediately after a stick of half a dozen or so bombs dropped out of its belly and scattered across the field. They exploded on impact, throwing up great clods of earth forty or fifty feet into the air. By now we had the canon pointing skywards and firing, and I blazed away for all it was worth but with little result. The bomber passed right overhead – the markings on its wings clearly visible – and then sped away and disappeared. I kept firing more out of hope than expectation.

Binbrook survived and, on 18 October, John was posted to wireless school where he passed an initial wireless course before progressing to Yatesbury, and the RAF No 2 Signal School to continue his training.

Situated in the heart of rural Wiltshire, Yatesbury was in many ways a 'typical' English village, surrounded by farmland. The RAF station was similarly typical of the period, a vast camp of drab brick-built accommodation blocks, flight offices, ablutions, and all manner of ancillary buildings required to cope with the throughput of hundreds of men every month.

The winter of 1940-41 was especially harsh, obliging many of the airmen to sleep with their greatcoats on and with as many blankets as they could find piled on top. The barracks comprised long, narrow rooms with rows of metal beds parked on either side, cold to the touch. At the end stood a single stove that seemed sufficient only to keep the ice from forming on the windows but little else.

The weather greatly restricted the flying training programme and increased the volume of ground instruction. John didn't mind; sitting in a warm classroom was infinitely more appealing than freezing in the rear of one of the De Havilland Dominie's that made up the Yatesbury Wireless Flight.

There was a camaraderie of glumness at Yatesbury; as well as the British (and Irish), there were also airmen from the Dominions – Canadians, Australians and New Zealanders – many of whom did not take kindly (or naturally) to RAF discipline, and would often fall foul of the RAF police. Complaints about the quality of the food were frequent, loud and often deserving.

Within weeks, John quickly became proficient in morse code, reaching the required eighteen words per minute with relative ease and quiet determination. Not only did he learn morse, but also the 'Q' code for communications, sending and receiving messages, and how to keep an accurate log. Although not technically minded, John applied himself diligently to any task he was set, and when the weather improved he was able to take his learning into the air and practice correct wireless procedure. This was still the early days of radio, before the wider introduction of Marconi radios and transmitters that transformed a lot of the wireless op:

> Our radio sets had coils, and in order to change frequency from perhaps medium to high, we had to pull out the medium coil and swap it for a high frequency coil before we could start listening or transmitting. This was easy enough on the ground but not so easy inside a small aircraft bumping around in a busy sky.

Having successfully navigated the first part of his WOP/AG training, John had yet another pause, with a posting to RAF Silloth on the Cumbrian coast (later an Operational Training Unit (OTU) for crews going on to Coastal Command). His duty was limited to communicating with local aircraft, and particularly listening out for any 'darkie' or 'mayday' calls to signal that an aircraft was lost or in distress.

John was at Silloth for less than a fortnight before a place became free at RAF Stormy Down at the end of April 1941 to attend No 7 Bombing & Gunnery School (7 B&GS) and commence his air gunnery course. It was a period for John of intense delight:

> *There were more classroom lectures on gunnery and gunnery practice, and of course we learned how to strip and rebuild a variety of different weapons, including the Browning .303s, such that we could do it blindfolded.*
>
> *We shot on the ranges and using cine guns, and in the air firing at a drogue. The tow aircraft were Fairey Battles, an obsolete, single engine monoplane bomber that had been annihilated by the Luftwaffe in May 1940 and quickly relegated to a training role where it could do less harm and kill fewer people.*
>
> *We would operate in pairs: one aircraft would tow the drogue while the pupils in the other aircraft would shoot at it; then we would swap. The pilots were nearly all Polish, and it would always make me smile when they came on intercom and said 'dropz the droguesz'".*
>
> *Firing at a drogue was not as easy as it sounds. With air gunnery you do not shoot directly at the target, but rather at the point in the sky where you expect the target to be when your bullets arrive, taking into account wind speed, air speed, bullet drop, angle of attack etc. and you had to get it right or you could shoot down the aircraft and not the drogue!*
>
> *One of the difficulties we had was in the type of weapons that we fired, including the drum-fed Lewis gun of First World War vintage. The Lewis[2] was a heavy, cumbersome affair (it weighed*

*28lbs / 14kg and was a little over 4ft long) and difficult to handle
in the air. It was also difficult to keep on target.*

Despite such challenges, John proved more than competent as an air
gunner and made good friends in the process.

*One of my best pals was Joe Brookes[3] from Birmingham. Joe was
perpetually miserable and constantly complaining, and we were
often paired up. He would especially mutter as we carried the
heavy ammunition drums for the Lewis guns out to the aircraft.
Despite his demeanour, I got to know Joe very well and grew to
like him, though it was a gradual process. After Stormy Down
our paths seemed to continually cross. He followed me out to the
Middle East (though to a different squadron), and later when I
returned to the UK to 4 Group out of Pocklington. When I was
awarded my Distinguished Flying Cross in March 1945, Joe's
name appeared in the same Gazette, the entry directly below my
own. By then he too was a flight lieutenant.*

By the end of June 1941, John had successfully completed his air
gunnery course, entitling him to wear the 'AG' half wing brevet above
his left side breast pocket and the sergeant's stripes on his sleeve, above
which sat the 'sparks' badge to denote that he was now a fully qualified
Wireless Operator/Air Gunner. Happily for John he also saw his pay
increased to twelve shillings a day, with an extra sixpence a day flying
pay.

For the third time in his brief training career, John was again given
a temporary posting to another RAF station, this time RAF Benson in
Oxfordshire (at the time part of 6 Group and home to an Operational
Training Unit), and again on ground defence duties. He was only there
a matter of days, however, before being posted to RAF Harwell on

5 July, a few miles up the road, to commence his own training for life on an operational squadron.

*   *   *

RAF Harwell had opened its doors for business in 1937, and by the time John arrived it had three concrete runways and four large hangars, as well as a host of administrative and ancillary buildings to house the hundreds of airmen who passed through its gates every month. It was officially home to 15 OTU, one of the very busiest in 6 Group, and equipped with the twin-engined Vickers Wellington medium bomber. Crews flew from Harwell and its satellite airfield, Mount Farm.

The first thing John noticed on arrival, having been transported from the small railway station at Didcot, was a sense of urgency that had been lacking in all of his training to date. Several aircraft were in the circuit to land and there was a general bustle to the place that suggested an air of impending action.

Before John had the chance to experience a Wellington, however, he first had more classroom lectures to refresh his knowledge, and a few hours in an Avro Anson to practice wireless procedure. He similarly loosed off a few more rounds on the range. When he did at last have the opportunity to clamber on-board a Wellington for the first time, he was immediately struck by the smell that was to become so reassuringly familiar in the months ahead. The geodetic design was also remarkable, in every sense of the word; a design that gave the Wimpey, as she was affectionately known, not only tremendous strength but also a unique and unmistakable character. It was not a type of aircraft that could be easily confused.

Having trained with his fellow 'trades' for the first few weeks (there were twenty wireless ops with a dual trade and a further ten 'pure' air gunners on the course), and flown with a variety of different pilots, John was then invited to find himself a crew.

The RAF at that time had a simple but incredibly effective method for the process known as 'crewing up', and it varied little from one OTU to another. Newly qualified pilots, navigators, wireless operators and air gunners were called to assemble in one of the hangars and invited to sort it out among themselves! Pilots would typically take the lead and find themselves a navigator, since the two would have to work closely as a pair. WOP/AGs who might have known one another from air gunnery school might also come together.

John was approached by a group of airmen who were almost complete, save for a front gunner. The two pilots, Ron Hodges and William Craig, and the observer Pilot Officer John Mahood were all commissioned men; the wireless operator and rear gunner – Robert Ralph and Reginald Van Walwyk – were NCOs. Since he liked the look of them, he 'volunteered' to take on responsibility for the front turret.

The next few weeks were spent getting to grips with the new aircraft and honing their skills as a crew. They were not totally exempt from more classroom exercises but the principal focus was in the air, conducting a series of cross-country exercises and practice bombing runs:

Flights were worked out for us. We would be given, for example, a three-hour cross country – the pupil navigator would be told the route, and had to work out our course, running time, etc – and then we would sit down and work out what to do as a crew.

Operational training was mainly of benefit to the pilot, as this was usually his first chance to fly the aircraft that he would use in battle. Often there was not much for me to do, other than learning about how to operate as a crew. Getting to grips with a larger aircraft was not easy and not every pilot was up to the task. We would not always go up together; the pilot would practise circuits and bumps with a 'screened' instructor, and only be allowed solo once the instructor was happy he was not going to wreck the aircraft. The Wellingtons at OTU were not the best; they were often worn out and battle weary, but they were all that we had and still in short supply, and it didn't do to crash one.

Training was not without its dangers. Many a promising young crew or highly experienced instructor were killed in accidents brought about by bad flying, bad aircraft or simply bad luck. On one night-exercise, John's training was nearly brought to a fatal halt by another enemy, bad weather:

We took off in the early evening and settled into the routine, the navigator giving our pilot the course on which to fly to reach a 'target' that we successfully found. On the return flight to Mount Farm, we ran into an electrical storm and conditions changed dramatically. I was in the front turret, and can clearly recall the sudden pitch-blackness that enveloped us and the rain lashing against the Perspex canopy. Then the intercom went dead and we couldn't speak to one another.

After being thrown around in the sky for quite some time, we finally emerged from the gloom and the navigator tried to fix our position. Obviously he didn't have a clue where we were for the next thing I know we are being fired upon by our flak. The nav had forgotten to switch on the Identification Friend or Foe (IFF), an electronic signal that would have told them we were on their side.

Happily the wireless operator managed to get his set working and put out a signal to say we were in distress. The routine then would be that a master searchlight would come on and act as a beacon to guide us to the nearest airfield to land. Our nearest base ended up being RAF Wyton in Cambridgeshire where we landed, low on fuel and high on adrenaline feeling rather lucky to be alive. We returned to base, somewhat sheepishly, the next day.

Casualties sustained at 15 OTU during the period August – October 1941 were in fact comparatively light compared to some other units. On 31 August, one of the most experienced instructors, Flight Lieutenant Ralph Alexander (soon after promoted squadron leader and awarded the AFC), almost came to grief when his Wellington lost an engine shortly after take-off. He used every one of his almost 3,000 flying hours to bring the stricken bomber safely back to earth without further damage to aircraft or crew. Two further crashes occurred the following month: on 16 September, Sergeant Arthur Patrick misjudged his landing, overshot, and came down among some bushes at the end of the runway. The 29-year-old Durham lad died from his injuries on the way to hospital; three nights later another Wellington was wrecked as it landed short of the runway, although this time the pilot escaped with his life.

The greatest tragedy came just a few days before John's departure, a crash with two senior instructors on board. The Wellington, flown by Flying Officer Leonard Boore DFM[4], was on late afternoon navigation exercise when, at very low height, a wing clipped the ground and the aircraft spun in. All of the crew were either injured or killed. The accident is somewhat unexplained given Boore's flying experience; he had been a pilot since 1935 and by the early winter of 1941 had some 1,200 hours to his name. He was lucky to survive. Not so fortunate was his fellow instructor, the observer, Fight Sergeant John Wilde DFM, who was killed in the resultant crash.

Harwell, as well as being an OTU, was also well known as a staging post for crews that were to be posted overseas. It had been instructed in the spring of 1941 to prepare fifteen crews each month to fly a Wellington to the Middle East, and in preparation for this role as well as the four standard 'Flights' (A, B, C & D), it also had a specific Ferry Training Flight.

Very much aware of this fact, and sensing his imminent departure, John popped the question to his Walls Factory girl Angela, and the two were married on 6 September 1941 in a small church in West Acton. A brief honeymoon was arranged courtesy of Angela's father, who had worked for a Norwegian shipping firm, and who owned a small yacht on the Thames.

The instructors were happy with the crew's progress, and the flight commander comfortable in signing off his pupil pilot as being ready for operations. John had flown around eighty hours, the majority of which had been practising at the set. No 43 Course had been 'a happy course', according to the end of term report, and the ten crews well above average in their ability. The Station Commander, Group Captain Percy Maitland MVO AFC, a former airship pilot,[5] felt that they would acquit themselves well in the Middle East[6]. But before then, there was one last rite of passage and one last test: a 'Nickel' raid over France.

'Nickelling' was the code word for dropping propaganda leaflets (and the odd 250lb bomb) over enemy territory as a small part in the wider psychological war that was being fought alongside the physical battles. Oftentimes given to new crews on joining a squadron, they were also briefed to novice crews coming towards the end of their training, and later in the war became very much part of the OTU syllabus. They gave crews their first taste of flying over enemy territory, and often their first experience of German searchlights and flak.

On 14 October, the crews of a small force of six 15 OTU Wellingtons were briefed to take part in 'Operation 34', a nickelling sortie to central France. All of the aircraft were instructed to 'Nickel' in the target area of Orleans, Dreux and Les Andeleys and then drop their bombs on enemy aerodromes. One of those six Wellingtons (Z8836) had John Brennan in the 'front' turret:

> *I remember very little about the operation, other than that there were six of us who set out and only four came back. We were all carrying leaflets as well as two 250lb general-purpose (GP) delayed-action bombs. It was a very long trip for an inexperienced crew, but I never gave a thought for those men who went missing. It didn't seem to affect me one way or another.*

It was certainly a long flight and not without its excitement. The first of the six aircraft was away at 18.30hrs and the last, Wellington Z8836, at 19.22hrs. Wing Commander Simpson (a senior officer for passing through operational training) ran into heavy flak in the area of Le Havre and returned with his bombs still on-board. Sergeant Lomas and his crew similarly had to contend with light flak, and on his journey home was 'coned' by friendly searchlights despite turning his IFF off and on.

They did have better luck with their bombs, however, hitting what they believed to be an airfield's flare path. After dropping his Nickels in the target area, Sergeant Wilson in Wellington R1769 also found and bombed an airfield at Vernouillet about two miles south of Dreux and narrowly missed being intercepted by a twin-engined enemy aircraft that first flew right in front of him and then tailed their Wellington for a good twenty-five minutes before finally being lost in the cloud. They made for Exeter and returned to Mount Farm a few hours later, landing at 05.30hrs. In his interrogation afterwards, Wilson reported the presence of a dummy airfield, seven miles to the west of the actual target.

In John's aircraft, the flight was a near-textbook operation. The pilots and observer worked together to find the target area, and identified and bombed an enemy airfield although no results could be seen because of thick cloud. They landed home safely at exactly 01.00hrs on the morning of the fifteenth.

Two aircraft, however, failed to return: Wellington R1275 and R1783 captained by Warrant Officer C. L. Humphreys and 23-year-old Sergeant Albert Beverley respectively. Both aircraft were tracked on their way out by Fighter Command but failed to return, most likely the result of enemy action. Of the twelve men, only Humphreys survived to become a prisoner of war.

Having successfully completed their first night time operation over France, the crew was prepared for the long-distance haul to the Middle East. This 'extra tuition' mainly comprised additional training for the observer, who would be expected to find Gibraltar – the first stage in their journey – having flown across hundreds of miles of unfamiliar skies and terrain. The track record for 15 OTU was encouraging: more than ninety per cent of all crews who set out for the Middle East arrived safely.[7] Although that meant that one in ten did not.

Against this background, John and his crew were told what to expect, and set out with confidence in their new Wellington for the short trip to Portreath in Cornwall from where their adventure would begin in earnest. They had each been given a week's pay in advance and a purse of French francs, just in case. The medical officer had also given them the once over, and the chief instructor had imparted their final orders and proffered a last few words of advice. HQ Fighter Command would be informed two hours before their expected departure. They did not want to get shot down by their own side. It was 17 October, and there was a red glow in the evening sky.

The portents were good.

Chapter 2

A Sunny Disposition

Fully re-fuelled and refreshed, the flight from Portreath to Gibraltar and the mighty Rock took a little over nine hours. It was a direct route to a point just clear of Brest, then southwest to Cape Finisterre and onward due south to Cape St Vincent, and what the Portuguese once thought of as the end of the world. From the cape, the pilot flew eastwards to Gib. The dangers were three-fold: German long-range fighters patrolling the Bay of Biscay; the unpredictable weather; and the inexperience of the crew. In the event the flight passed without incident: the weather was benign; the Germans appeared disinterested; and the crew was sufficiently trained to arrive in one piece. Only the landing gave John cause for concern:

> *Gibraltar only has one runway and it's not particularly long. Get the approach wrong and you could end up either in Spain or in the drink! As it happens, our skipper made a perfectly respectable job of it and with one short hop and a skip we were down.*

German spies across the border in La Linea, brazenly peering through powerful binoculars or telescopes from a tall tower on a hill overlooking the bay, had noted their arrival and, more importantly, would note their departure; arguably, the most dangerous part of their journey was yet to begin. But for more than two weeks, John and his crew were delayed on the Rock, with very little to buy in the shops and even less to do other than while their time away sightseeing, sleeping or playing cards. Even the famous monkeys could do little to distract or amuse.

At last, on 7 November, they were briefed for the next stage of their journey, and another potentially dangerous long 'hop' to the beleaguered island of Malta in the Mediterranean. It was a flight of more than 1,300 miles, right at the limit of the Wellington's endurance[1]:

We took off in the very early morning and set course for Malta and I was again in the front turret. The conditions in the first part of the flight were ideal. It was a cloudless sky, and I could clearly see the sea shimmering below me in the sunlight. It was such a beautiful sight that it was hard to imagine there was a war on. At one point, if I looked hard enough, I could just about make out the outline of the North African coast away to starboard.

The real danger came as we approached the volcanic island of Pantelleria, a small island in the straits of Sicily that was almost half way between Sicily and North Africa and past which we would need to fly to reach Malta. Before reaching Pantelleria we were to drop to below 1,000ft so as to avoid detection from enemy radar. We knew that there were squadrons of Italian and German fighters close by, but perhaps somewhat closer than we thought.

Then, as I peered out in front of me, I thought I saw a speck in the sky. I blinked and looked again. It was still there, only the speck seemed to get steadily bigger. It was not a smudge on the Perspex or some other trick of the eye. Then there was no mistaking it was another aircraft, and it was closing fast. Recalling the hours spent on aircraft recognition, I identified it as a single-seat Messerschmitt Bf109, Germany's best fighter, and making its way straight towards us in a head on attack.

I lined the fighter up in my sites, released the safety catches on the guns, and called to the pilot to take evasive action. I then squeezed both triggers and opened fire.

John's twin Browning .303 machine guns spat out a steady stream of bullets in the direction of the oncoming fighter. Every fifth round loaded in the belts was a 'tracer' so that the gunner could literally 'see' the trajectory of his bullets and adjust his aim accordingly. With a rate of fire of 1,150 rounds a minute, assuming there were no jams, the bomber could put up an apparently fearsome defence, though the range and hitting power of the .303s was nothing compared to the 20mm canon of the attacking Messerschmitt.

John held his fingers on the triggers and gave the enemy a long burst but seemingly without effect. The fighter flashed by and described a large arc in the sky as it turned to attack again, this time from the rear. The rear gunner, Reg Van Walwyk, now had his chance, as the captain threw the Wellington into a series of tight turns:

The pilot took terrific evasive action that must have gone on for a couple of minutes but actually went by in a flash. I kept blazing away, the smell of cordite from the spent cartridges filling my nostrils and the brass cases falling around my feet and onto the floor. By now I had fired off many hundreds of rounds and then, almost as suddenly as it had begun, it was over. The fighter broke off the attack and again became little more than a speck in the sky as it disappeared. He was probably low on fuel, and it had certainly been a lucky escape.

It took some time before calm was restored and they could be sure that there were no other fighters in the area. The pilot asked the navigator for a position and received a blunt response. He had been somewhat pre-occupied and needed time to gather his maps and charts that were now strewn across his desk and on the floor. Only at length was the navigator able to gain an accurate fix, and give the pilot a new course to steer.

Now the rest of the crew took stock. Despite the ferocity of the attack, no-one was hurt and there appeared to be no damage to the aircraft. The engines were still humming their re-assuring tune and the aircraft was responding well to the controls. The only concern now was fuel.

The pilot had pushed the throttles fully forward to get every last ounce of speed out of the bomber during the attack but that had consumed vast amounts of critical fuel. They still had another 150 miles or so to go, at least another hour of flying time, and it would be touch and go as to whether they would make it.

John was the first to see the island dead ahead, a small oasis of land in a calm of blue with its distinctive shape and rocky outcrops and cliffs that became more discernible the closer they flew.

John had been perched on his seat, such as it was, for almost nine hours, and he couldn't wait to be on terra firma once again. The adrenaline that had earlier pumped through his veins had long since gone, and now he was both mentally tired and physically exhausted.

The wireless operator called Malta control to obtain a final bearing and permission to land. Then came the snag:

The pilot asked for permission to land only to be told 'didn't he bloody well know that there was an air raid on'? Of course we did, as we could see a number of other aircraft about the place, but our need was desperate. The controller told us to do a 'dog leg' but the pilot calmly refused. He told the controller that our petrol situation was critical and that we were coming in to land.

The skipper went straight in without any fancy stuff and made a good approach, lowering his undercarriage and flaps. I could see various aircraft way overhead that I took to be German bombers but well out of range. The skipper held the bomber off the ground as we reduced speed, the runway racing away below me.

Then, just as we were about to touch down there was a terrific bang and a 'crump' as a stick of bombs exploded terrifyingly close by and our aircraft was involuntarily lifted into the sky and onto its back. For the briefest of moments we seemed to hang in the air until there was another terrifically loud bang and the scraping of metal as the aircraft came to a halt the wrong way up. We had been completely flipped over.[2]

Badly shaken, the crew took some moments before again regaining their composure. Then at last they were able to scramble clear, dazed and confused, choking and spitting from the dust in the air. Happily, they had not been carrying bombs or else the Wellington would have undoubtedly exploded with them inside. Outside of the aircraft there was an eerie silence. The German bombers had gone, their droning engines already faded in the distance, and the men seemed to be standing on their own on what looked like a deserted airfield. Nothing and no-one moved to help them; it was as though they had landed from outer space.

Gathering themselves together they headed quickly for a small cluster of buildings that looked like a shanty village, but they took to be flying control, and reported their arrival, lest they hadn't been noticed. The reception was none too warm: aircraft were in desperately short supply, and the crew had failed to deliver theirs in one piece. Worst than that, it was now blocking the runway and a danger to other aircraft. It was not an auspicious start to their Middle Eastern tour and the pilot was beginning to regret his decision not to do as the controller had instructed.

John had only been vaguely aware of the plight of Malta from the newsreels, but now he could see the devastation for himself: buildings with no roofs; the twisted remains of shapes that were once aircraft, skeletal ghosts beside an airfield pockmarked with craters.

The island had been under attack since the summer of 1940 and the locals had already endured almost eighteen months of constant aerial bombardment. After the invasion of Crete in May 1941, many had supposed that Malta would be next. And for good reason. While it remained in Allied hands, it could be a constant thorn in the Axis side, a floating airbase in the Mediterranean from which the RAF could launch a series of attacks against enemy forces in North Africa and Italy, and destroy their shipping. For many reasons, the Germans were dissuaded from invasion, perhaps fearing the tremendous casualties that would no doubt result. Operation Mercury, the assault on Crete, had been a stunning success but the cost in human lives had been too high.

Malta relied on convoys to provide its forces with ammunition, aviation fuel, and above all, food. Despite the heroic efforts of the Royal Navy and their Merchant Navy contemporaries, by the end of 1941, and John's arrival, fears of starvation were fast in danger of becoming a reality. And things were about to get worse.

In late November, Field Marshal Kesselring, the Axis Commander in Chief for the South, was told by the Fuhrer personally to abandon any thoughts of invasion, but to focus his efforts on literally bombing the island and its heroic defenders into submission. It was the start of a new horror.

Without an aircraft, John and his crew were effectively stranded. Shortly after the All Clear sounded, a small army of men emerged from their hiding places to descend like a proverbial plague of locusts on the Wellington and strip her bare of anything that might be of use, including all of the crew's rations and most of their personal kit. Nothing remained.

From the airfield, the crew were eventually taken into the ancient city of Valetta, and accommodated in a building, appropriately enough, known as the poor house. It had no roof.

> *We stayed in Malta for a little over a fortnight, living in limbo. No-one was very interested in us and we were not particularly interested in them. We certainly had nothing to do with any of the locals, some of who were stick-thin and clearly starving. Food was in desperately short supply and it seemed to us that the island was on its last legs. Little did we know how close they would come later to surrender and defeat.*
>
> *My memory of Malta is primarily one of spending almost the entire day dodging in and out of air raids, finding anywhere we could to take cover, such as it was. At night our sleep was also constantly interrupted by the sirens heralding yet another attack. It was a most uncomfortable existence, but no doubt even more so for the locals.*

The crew's stay on Malta came to an end when they were informed that a Catalina flying boat would take them on the next stage of their journey to Alexandria. The trip was something of a pleasure cruise after the previous few weeks and they were glad when the boat landed in the harbour at Alexandria and a small motorboat arrived alongside to take them off. As a crew they then entrained to the Canal Zone, and from there were taken by RAF transport to the permanent base at Shallufa.

Shallufa was situated near to the Ports of Suez and Tewfik, and the headquarters of 257 Wing, comprising the Wellington-equipped 37 and 38 Squadrons. Both had been in the Middle East since the end of 1940, and had recently been operating against targets in Libya, Sicily and southern Italy. Shallufa was otherwise unremarkable, except for a neighbouring compound that housed several hundred Italian prisoners of war who, John observed, appeared to live in better conditions and in greater comfort than their British guards!

John, as an NCO, was assigned to a tent, whereas the officers were quartered within the permanent buildings. The Bedouin lifestyle was something he was going to have to get used to. He was kitted out with summer shirts and shorts, and the next day ordered to parade for the short trip to another RAF station at Kabrit, the home to 148 Squadron and his first operational posting.

This time he went alone.

Chapter 3

A Class Apart

John was somewhat surprised to be parted from his crew but excited at the prospect of joining a squadron with a proud and established reputation in the Middle East.

Formed on 10 February 1918 as a night bomber unit operating FE2bs, the Squadron got off to a difficult start when one of its number crashed in the Channel on the journey across to France. The pilot was rescued by a passing French trawler.

Flying from the airfield at Auchel, the squadron immediately found itself thrown into the thick of the action, supporting the Allies to repel the last German offensive of the First World War in the spring of 1918. Night bombing of enemy aerodromes, railheads and billets were the order of the day, although it was itself bombed out of its home on 3 May, four were killed and several others wounded, as well as losing most of its stores. Under the command throughout by Major I.T. Lloyd, among its more notable pilots was Captain L. P. 'Don' Watkins, a Canadian awarded the military cross (MC) earlier in the war for destroying a Zeppelin near Saxmunden in Norfolk.

By the time that war had ended, the squadron had dropped more than 120 tons of bombs for the loss of only two machines. It was soon after disbanded and only reformed at Scampton in 1937 as a long-range medium bomber squadron under the command of Squadron Leader Richard Kellett[1]. Still, at that time, equipped with a bi-plane for bombing operations, within weeks its Audax bombers had been replaced by the long-range Vickers Wellesley. A move to Stradishall and a change of role to heavy night-time bombing the following year meant the squadron re-equipped with Handley Page Heyford IIIs, by then under the command of Squadron Leader Harold Haines DFC (later Air Commodore H. A. Haines CBE, DFC. He won his DFC serving in North Russia in 1919). By the time war was declared, it had received the first of its Wellington Is and moved to Harwell in Berkshire.

Designated a Group Pool Squadron, the unit received eight Avro Ansons to assist in producing its quota of twelve trained bomber crews every six weeks. Re-designated 15 OTU, the squadron ceased to exist until it was again reformed on 30 April, before then being disbanded the following month. It was not until December of the same year that the Squadron once again reformed from detachments of 38, 99 and 115 Squadrons, then based at Luqa in Malta.

The Squadron operated from Malta for four months, flying 138 sorties comprising some 434 operational hours and dropping 284,000lbs of bombs. It was evacuated to Egypt on 23 March 1941, the main bulk of the squadron sailing on HMS *Bonaventure*. It spent several months being brought back up to strength, command of the Squadron passing from Wing Commander E.C 'Sparrow' Lewis (OC from 4 March 1941 having himself taken over command from Squadron Leader Foss) to Squadron Leader – later wing commander – Frederick 'Turkey' Rainsford. It seemed the squadron had a penchant for bird-based nicknames!

By the end of 1941, at around the same time that John arrived at Kabrit, the Squadron had dropped a further 1,763,960lbs of explosive on enemy targets and was operating at maximum capacity. Indeed, the ORB diary entry for 19 November makes a point of stating that it had eighteen aircraft serviceable for operations, but only seventeen crews.

The truck in which John was travelling trundled through the main gate at which point there was a brief conversation and the usual checks were made as to the occupants' identities. Satisfied, the barrier was raised slowly and the truck carried on its journey along the dusty road to the main headquarters building, a drab non-descript affair, for John to report his arrival:

> *I don't know why I was travelling alone or why they decided to split up the crew. Clearly they were short of an air gunner so I was posted as a 'spare bod' to make up the numbers. Having met the orderly sergeant and the adjutant, I was told to report to the Gunnery Leader where I would receive further instruction.*[2]

The squadron had received a good number of new crews and spare bods in the previous weeks, as well as re-mustering several airmen into aircrew, to make up for an unfortunate run of casualties that had seen too many very experienced men killed or missing in action.

On 29 October, the Squadron lost two aircraft and two crews in a single night. Both had set off to attack shipping in Candia and Suda Bay, and only one of the pilots (Flying Officer Norman Canton DFC) survived to become a prisoner of war, having first been sheltered by Cretans before inevitably being captured.

Worse was to follow two nights later when ten aircraft (seven from 'A' Flight and three from 'B' Flight) were briefed for operations against Benghazi, a much favoured and frequent target of the time. Half of their number crashed on return, the result, it appears, of a ground mist. Seven aircrew were injured, at least four of them seriously. The Squadron had therefore lost sixteen men in less than three days – eleven killed, four injured and one languishing in a German Stalag.

And their bad luck didn't stop there. A 25-year-old Australian pilot, Pilot Officer Hugh McMaster was killed with three of his crew on an air test. They had been accepting a new Wellington II to the Squadron. Four of the new Mark had recently been delivered and promised a much better performance than the workhorse 1Cs. But there was a downside. Whereas the Pegasus engine of the 1C was air cooled, the Merlin of the Mk II required glycol, and glycol could leak. McMaster's aircraft stalled after the port engine cut out, crashed and burst into flames. McMaster had completed no fewer than forty-two operations and was an experienced flyer. He was also married, and left a widow in Queensland.

A week later, on the night of 12 November, two more experienced crews were lost over Benghazi, and a third Wellington was lost on the night of 16 November. This latter aircraft was flown by one of the squadron's more senior pilots, in experience rather than age: 21-year-old Flight Lieutenant Robert Gordon.

Gordon's aircraft was seen to be hit by heavy flak and brought down near the target. Gordon had been with the Squadron for more than a year, and recently awarded the Distinguished Flying Cross. He was flying his sixty-first raid in a Wellington aircraft. Described as 'the most popular and brilliant pilot on the Squadron', Gordon also had one of the most experienced crews: his observer, Flying Officer Peter Bitmead was on his fortieth trip; Sergeant Dennis Pickerill, Sergeant Ronald Murphy and Flight Sergeant Angus Hunter already had forty operations to their names. The sixth man of the crew, Sergeant David Clark, was just short of double figures.

Another accident caused by yet another engine failure led to the deaths of two more airmen on the night of 28 November. This time both engines cut while the aircraft was at only 800ft, the Canadian second pilot and the front gunner being killed in the resulting crash. A full court of enquiry was held into whether the crash had been caused by an ingress of water in the fuel.

November ended as it had begun, with yet another loss and another accident. Pilot Officer Bill Astell was returning from a raid on Benghazi. On his approach to land at an advanced landing ground (ALG) he failed to notice another aircraft that had jumped ahead of him and stayed at the end of the flare path. Astell only spotted the aircraft as he was about to touch down and frantically tried to go round again. With insufficient speed the port wing dropped, touched the ground and was wrenched off from the wing root. The aircraft swung and burst into flames causing several nasty injuries to the crew, including the skipper. Astell was badly burned on his back and suffered a fractured skull and a head wound that needed thirty-two stitches. Also hurt was his navigator, Sergeant Stephen Geary, with damage to his spine. Geary had only days before been awarded an immediate Distinguished Flying Medal (DFM), having completed more than seventy operations, nearly all of them in daylight.

Bill Astell was just one of a notable band of pilots and personalities within 148 Squadron that distinguished themselves in the Middle East and subsequently. A Mancunian by birth, Astell had joined the RAFVR in 1939 and completed his flying training in Zimbabwe (then Rhodesia). After operational training at 70 OTU for service in the Middle East, he was posted to 148 Squadron in January 1941 and was coming to the end of his first tour. (He would later return to the UK and begin a second tour of operations with 57 Squadron, before being plucked to join a special squadron to drop an equally special bouncing bomb on the dams in the Ruhr.)

Alec Cranswick was another who stood out, and another who was coming to the end of an arduous tour in the Middle East. Cranswick had almost literally been born to fly, his father having been a pilot who lost his life in a collision in 1928 when practicing for the annual RAF Display at Hendon. He had joined 148 Squadron from 214 and flown operations from Malta, and by March 1941 he had completed forty-six trips. Taken off operations, he suffered a serious bout of scarlet fever while 'resting' before again being posted to join 148 at Kabrit in October. (Cranswick was awarded the DFC in April 1942, his citation then praising his sixty-one sorties over Germany and enemy-held territory and added the Distinguished Service Order (DSO) the following summer for service 'worthy of the highest praise'. As part of Pathfinder Force (PFF), the elite squadrons that led every major bombing operation from August 1942 onwards, Cranswick took his total number of operations to more than 100 before finally losing his life on the night of 4 July 1944.)

The man who would turn out to be John's Flight Commander was a similarly interesting personality, though his style of leadership – described on occasion as 'unconventional' – divided opinion. Squadron Leader, The Honourable Robert Baird, known inevitably as 'Jock' because of his Scottish heritage, was the son of a former Governor General of Australia and every inch a product of the Empire. Posted originally to 70 Squadron, he had joined 148 shortly prior to John's arrival and instantly made an impression. He appeared intolerant of any man that wasn't prosecuting the war with the same level of urgency and vigour as his own.[3]

And it was not just among the pilots that the squadron enjoyed its share of characters. Closer to John's own 'trade' was one of the senior air gunners, and a qualified gunnery leader, Leonard 'Tubby' Vaughan. Tubby had been a fighter pilot in the First World War with more than 900 hours to his name and, at 43, was awarded a DFC for 'courage, determination, and devotion to duty'. His citation credited him with fifty-four operations, including twenty-eight against Germany and German-occupied territory. He was every bit the 'father' figure of his crew, Tubby and his pilot being once described by a visiting war correspondent to much hilarity as 'father and son!'. (Vaughan would later be promoted flight lieutenant and add a DSO to his DFC with 40 Squadron before being killed as a passenger in a Halifax which crashed taking off from Luqa in December 1942.)

John was directed to a dispersal on the far side of the airfield and told to find his skipper. It was hot, and he was not in any particular hurry:

I approached one of the Wellingtons but there didn't appear to be anyone about. I went to the front of the aircraft and climbed the metal ladder under the nose to be greeted with the sight of my pilot with a dustpan and brush in his hands, cleaning out the cockpit. He looked at me and said, in a very plummy accent, 'welcome aboard Brennan'. It was one of the few occasions he ever addressed me by name.

John's new captain was Pilot Officer Donald Crossley, who gave the impression of being a classic example of the British Public School system. Donald Marshall Crossley, to give him his full title, spoke to his new air gunner in much the same way as John imagined he might address his fag, valet or chauffer. It was perhaps not surprising. Crossley was every inch the young gentleman born with the silver spoon in his mouth. At Harrow he had been a monitor in The Head Master's, one of the most senior boys in the school, and excelled at gymnastics where he had been champion in 1931. He was also in the first XI and XV respectively for football and rugby and always seemed destined for higher service.

It was not a comfortable meeting. Crossley was an officer; John was an NCO. They were polar opposites. Crossley was, literally, to the manor born, and the skipper seemed determined to ensure the social gulf that existed between the two men should be re-enforced rather than broken down.

Other faces started to appear including that of the observer, another officer, Pilot Officer Lance Baron. Baron was an Oxford graduate, and appeared to take his lead from his captain. Both pilot and navigator were aloof, almost to the point of rudeness. John felt disappointed; it was not a happy introduction to squadron life.

Later in the war, much later, and particularly among the heavy bomber squadrons in the UK, many of the crews would tend to the stick together. Although officers and NCOs had to mess separately, and eat and sleep apart, in the aircraft and when off duty they operated as one. They would drink together, laugh together, love together and, if necessary, die together. But that single sense of camaraderie was not universal. Many of the captains of aircraft in the first two years of the war were still regular servicemen, with regular views on rank and hierarchy. The concept of mixing socially with their NCO aircrew, certainly not for them. Later there would be journeymen commissioned pilots, in for the duration, and not necessarily steeped in the traditions or prejudices of 'us and them'. Later too, some of the officers had started life as sergeant pilots and had been commissioned, either because of experience, or sometimes through dead men's shoes. Either way they had experienced both sides of the divide, and were less affected in their bearing and attitude to their fellow travellers.

Happily for John, not all of the crew were officers. He received a much warmer greeting from the wireless operator and rear gunner, Dougie Moore and 'Jock' Hutchinson, both of whom were sergeants like him, and neither of whom seemed bothered by social graces. 'Jock', it appeared, already had a number of operations under his belt, and had taken part in raids on Germany earlier in the war. His experience was much in demand, and he was especially kind to new or inexperienced gunners joining the squadron.

With the introductions completed, John returned to the main building to seek out the stores, and draw bedding and blankets. He was also issued with Khaki battledress of the type worn by the army. It was meant to provide better camouflage against the desert, should he be shot down. He was also issued with his escape kit, such as it was, comprising a silk escape map of the Egyptian Western Desert and Libyan Cyrenaica, some French francs and what was known locally as a 'Goolie chit' in case of being shot down and captured by Arabs.

The Goolie chit was a throwback from an earlier war when Royal Flying Corps pilots in India and Mesopotamia needed security in the form of a document that promised a reward to anyone who would bring an unharmed British aviator back to British lines. It was so called because local tribesmen in the area were said to turn over aviators to their womenfolk, who castrated them for use as servants (and so they would lose their 'goolies').

This chit was a letter, or cloth-mounted certificate, bearing the British Government's coat of arms and text printed in English and Arabic that read:

> *To all Arab Peoples – Greetings and Peace be upon you. The bearer of this letter is an Officer of the British Government and a friend to all Arabs. Treat him well, guard him from harm, give him food and drink, help him to the nearest British soldiers and you will be rewarded. Peace and Mercy of God upon you. The British High Command in the East.*

As well as the script, it also included some helpful tips on local customs:

> *Remove footwear on entering their tents. Completely ignore their women. If thirsty, drink the water they offer but do NOT fill your water bottle from their personal supply / Go to their well and fetch what you want. Never neglect any puddle or other water supply for topping up your bottle. Use the Halazone[4] included in your Aid box. Do not expect breakfast if you sleep the night. Arabs will give you a mid-day or evening meal. Remember – never try and hurry in the desert, slow and sure does it.*

To be shot down and captured by the Arabs was a sobering thought for a young man from Ireland or indeed any man who wanted to keep his genitals intact. John was in for more of a surprise when he grabbed a lift to the NCO's accommodation:

The officers were billeted in comfortable headquarters and in wooden buildings next to the officers' mess on the main camp site. So too were the regular airmen who serviced and maintained the aircraft. But for the NCO aircrew, we had something of a surprise in store.

About four or five hundred yards from the airfield was what I can only described as a tented village, a sprawling mass of canvas that seemed to go on forever. There must have been literally hundreds of tents, all pegged into scrapings in the rocky sand to offer some protection against the wind and also from enemy air attack. I was allocated a tent and a hole and quickly realised that this would be my home for the foreseeable future.

Each of the tents had been sprinkled with creosote so that the sand would stick to it and make them more difficult to spot by any passing German aircraft. As well as the smaller tents were larger ones that doubled as the sergeants' mess and dining hall. There was also a communal shower, an ablution 'block' fed by a single water pipe to serve more than a hundred men. John, who was used to having little while growing up, was somewhat taken aback by the paucity of facilities, but soon settled in:

Sleeping on the ground was not an option; it was too cold and too uncomfortable. So once I had got to know my way around a little I fashioned my own bed by acquiring a stretcher and mounting it on four gallon cans, one at each corner. I smothered each of the cans with creosote at the base to stop any unwelcome visitors from crawling into my bed during the night. I then put the straw palliasse on top and covered it in blankets to make it more comfortable.

Close to our 'village' was an army training area with the troops being put through their paces. Later we learned that they were part of Stirling's Special Air Service (SAS) men. Closer to home, the NCO in the neighbouring tent was Calvert-Fisher who had been with me at OTU and was part of Mickey Vertican's crew. My abiding memory of Calvert-Fisher was that he never stopped talking, and would sit at breakfast with a large bowl of cereal balanced on an ammunition box and chat about anything. He was intelligent, well-read (and I think privately-educated) and I enjoyed our conversations.

Now settled in, John turned his attentions to the war.

*   *   *

From the moment the Italian troops marched confidently into Egypt in 1940, the war in the western desert had ebbed and flowed. The Allies' army of the Nile, led brilliantly by Generals Wavell and O'Connor, saw to it that the Italians' confidence was short-lived, routing their forces and advancing as far as El Agheila by February of the following year. Soon after, however, the Allies were denuded of men and material, hastily despatched to counter the German invasion of Greece, and many squandered in the defence of Crete. The arrival of Erwin Rommel and his much vaunted Afrika Korps at much the same time spelled disaster for the weakened Allied forces. The Allies were steadily pushed back to the Egyptian border, leaving a small pocket of resistance at the port of Tobruk – a garrison of Australian, British, and Polish troops who would win deserved fame for the dogged determination in resisting the relentless German siege. Only in November 1941 was that garrison finally relieved as the renamed Eighth Army embarked on Operation Crusader and reached El Agheila for a second time while the Desert

Fox retreated in good order. Re-armed and re-supplied, and with superior weaponry – especially in relation to tanks – Rommel was now on the verge of launching his counter-offensive.

Although Allied equipment was arguably outclassed on the ground, in the air the RAF suffered no such shortcomings. At Kabrit, 148 Squadron was fully up to strength. It had only recently become part of the newly-formed 205 (Heavy Bomber) Group, comprising five squadrons in all (37, 38, 70, 108 and 148) under the command of Air Commodore Lachlan MacLean MC. MacLean was an officer of considerable energy and talent who had learned to fly as early as 1913. He was very much the right man for the job.

Each of the 205 Group squadrons was equipped with the Wellington, and the arrival of the Wellington IIs at Kabrit led to an increase in flying activity as the pilots put their new aircraft through their paces. The squadron also received a new supply of ordinance, including the first 4,000lb bombs, huge beasts described in the 148 Squadron ORB as being '12ft long and 3ft across'[5].

In support of Operation Crusader, the heavy bombers had been busy. Their main duty was to disrupt and destroy the enemy supply system, principally by bombing the ports through which the supplies were transported. Their second main responsibility was to disrupt the activities of the Axis air force, both the German Luftwaffe and Italian Regia Aeronautica, to destroy their airfields and keep their fighters, bombers and reconnaissance aircraft on the ground and in harm's way.

Vast quantities of food, ammunition and fuel were needed to keep the German forces supplied. Typically, these were shipped across from Italy to Tripoli, and thence by smaller coastal vessels to Benghazi. Derna was often used as a staging post between the bustling port and the front line. Not surprisingly, both would feature heavily in the list of potential targets. Indeed the bombing of Benghazi became so frequent as to be referred to as 'the mail run' and the men made up songs about it.[6]

Bombing operations had evolved into a set routine. In the late afternoon, the crews would assemble for briefing, a relatively casual affair that bore no resemblance to the set-piece events of later years, where a curtain was drawn back to reveal the 'target for tonight'. The Intelligence Officer (IO) did his best however, drawing up blackboard displays of the target and its defences, detailing known searchlights and flak, and preparing route and target maps for the navigators. A short, five-minute description of the target was usually given, and its importance fully articulated.

Given the distance of some of the targets, the RAF established a small number of Advanced Landing Grounds (ALGs), primarily in the Daba area, up to a distance of some 450 miles west of Kabrit; they could not be called airfields as they were little more than a scraping in the ground. The Wellingtons, with a full bomb load onboard, would fly to their allocated ALG to be refuelled for the onward journey. After any last minute intelligence had been imparted, the crews would then set off into the night to do their bidding:

ALG060 was one of our most frequent stop-overs, a flat hard surface that had once been a river bed and about 200 miles or so from our base. Landing a fully loaded Wellington on such a surface was always dicey, even when it was well swept, and certainly caused me more than a few anxious moments, especially when carrying a 'blockbuster'.

At each landing ground there were a handful of tents and a few lonely but extremely hard working ground crew and an officer to oversee events. They would put out a temporary flare path at night using goose-neck flares to guide us in. We did not have such things as bowsers or other vehicles to move supplies or aircraft. The

Wellington fuel tanks had to be topped up by hand using jerry cans and muscle. It was an exhausting task, particularly in the extremes of bad weather that we sometimes experienced in the desert.

We would usually arrive in the early evening, and be off again around eight, but this could vary depending on the target. We would help the ground crews to make our aircraft ready, and then enjoy a pre-op meal of Maconochie's stew comprising sliced turnips, carrots and potatoes in a thin soup of dubious heritage. If we were lucky, we'd eat our stew with a dog biscuit, and wash it all down with a small canteen of water which, as you can imagine, was closely rationed.

If all went well, we would return to the landing ground mid-morning where we would be preliminarily debriefed before flying on home.

Crossley's first operation after John's arrival was on 23 November, when three aircraft from A Flight set off and attacked Benghazi. All returned safely after a seven-hour trip. A further operation to El Aden followed on 4 December and to Gazala on 7 December, both flown in Wellington W5555 – a Wellington II. Before the month was out, the crew completed at least five more operations, including a six-hour trip to El Agheila and another seven-hour 'mail run'.

Bomb loads varied: 500lb and 250lb bombs and incendiaries were familiar and favoured. Occasionally there were mines to be carried too. When the aircraft was bombed up with one of the precious 4,000 pounders however, the crew was given specific instructions as to what to do if they suffered a 'hang up':

The 'blockbusters', as we called them, had very sensitive detonators and had to be secured in the bomb bay by means of a special cable. This increased the chances of having a 'hang up' when the bombs refused to release. If this happened, we were told under no circumstances to attempt a landing, but rather to bail out!

When they were successfully released, however, you could feel the aircraft 'lift' as the enormous weight fell from its belly, and at night, when they exploded, you could clearly see the flash from heights of 10,000ft or more. They did great damage.

Sunday, 7 December 1941 was of course a propitious day, although it would take a little while before the news reached the landing grounds. The Japanese attack on the American fleet at Pearl Harbor brought a new and fearsome enemy, but an even greater ally with a subsequent declaration of war by the US on the entire Axis of evil. It was also the date of a remarkable incident on the squadron and one that left a lasting impression.

The stresses and strains of air combat manifested themselves in many different ways. For some, it could be the start of a twitch, a tic, or the scratch of an imaginary itch. Small disagreements could quickly escalate into major rows. It could be more serious: an early return perhaps as the result of imagined engine trouble, though with the Wellington engine problems were a familiar occurrence. Some were so debilitated and exhausted that they became ill. A big issue was boredom, leaving the men with time to brood:

Boredom could be dangerous and on base there was little or nothing to do, apart from the occasional swim in the Bitter Lake. We lived like monks; there was the occasional beer for those who wanted it (I personally didn't drink) but little else and the food was very poor. We had sweet potatoes with virtually every meal and I have always detested them. We were a long way from home and felt very isolated. Many had already flown a huge amount of trips with no end in sight. We flew, we ate, we slept and the next day we did it all again. It is no surprise to me that occasionally somebody cracked.

Men began to complain about fatigue, even after only half a dozen trips or so. The CO's response was a pep talk and a quiet word with their flight commanders. Sometimes it wasn't enough. Two sergeants (McIntosh and Stone) were removed from operational flying and, after undergoing a medical board, were recommended for discharge from the service on the grounds that they had 'lost the CO's confidence' and 'did not possess the qualities expected of a member of an aircrew.' McIntosh had flown seven operations and Stone seventeen. They were the first cases of what was shamefully called LMF – Lacking in Moral Fibre. They'd had enough.

John remembers another incident at the other extreme, relating to one of the senior air gunners – senior in both rank and in age. Flight Lieutenant George Culley was approaching 50. He'd seen action in the First World War, originally with the Norfolk Regiment in 1914-15 as a lieutenant in the machine gun corps (MGC). Transferring to the Royal Flying Corps in 1916 he had flown a number of the top aircraft of the time, including the De Havilland 5 (DH5) and the Sopwith Pup. By the end of the war he had qualified as an SE5 pilot, one of the best Allied aircraft then available, before finally retiring from the RAF (as the RFC became on 1 April 1918) in 1919.

During the inter-war years he passed his solicitor's exams and practiced in Cardiff. With the outbreak of the Second World War he re-joined the RAF, initially (perhaps given his age) in the administrative and special duties branch before being assigned to general duties and qualifying as an air gunner.

No-one could doubt Culley's commitment to the cause; what was in doubt, however, was his mental wellbeing. On the morning of 7

December, Culley took it upon himself to enter one of the squadron pilots, Flying Officer Wallace Watson, into the authorisation book as detailed to fly on operations that night, and entered himself as one of the crew. When confronted by his flight commander, of equal rank, he became rather annoyed, giving Baird no option other than to report the incident to the CO.

Rainsford was not impressed, but sensitive to Culley's position. While he sympathised with the air gunner's determination, he knew that Culley had gone too far, and openly challenged the authority of his immediate superior. Culley was congratulated on his fine record, and told that he would be rested from operations with immediate effect. Unfortunately, this did little to appease the older man. Like an admonished schoolboy, Culley informed his squadron commander that he had no intention of returning home, or obeying his order, and walked out of the room and across to his aircraft to sit in the rear turret.

At this point the adjutant became involved, and again tried to reason with him but to no avail. Culley steadfastly refused to budge, and the CO was once again called, the adjutant now fearing Culley's mental health. Rainsford ordered Culley to get out of the turret; Culley became angry and refused to do so. Ultimately the CO was given no option other than to call the guard and place the wayward flight lieutenant under close arrest. He was escorted to his room and held under lock and key with an armed guard placed outside his door. Two days later he was taken to HQ Middle East to attend a medical board.

Culley's case is unusual but by no means unique. At that time there appeared to be no agreed 'tour' system – aircrew simply flew until they were exhausted or they were killed. Rainsford was informed by HQ 205 Group to provide returns for personnel who were 'operationally tired' and did so, often, in the latter stages of his tenure. But this list was often down to his individual judgment and the advice of his flight commanders and the medical officer (MO). It was not based, it seems, on the number of operational hours flown, nor the number of sorties. Some were selected after circa forty operations; others not until they had reached seventy or more. Their experience, however, was essential, not only for the proficiency of the squadron in which they served, but also as instructors for the rapidly expanding numbers of operational training units being established back home.

The danger of crews potentially losing their nerve was certainly not ignored. An entry into the ORB for 15 December discusses the squadron aircraft detailed for mining operations (ie the dropping of mines to cause damage to enemy shipping) against Benghazi. It states clearly that the High Command does not appreciate the strain that aircrew are put under by having to wait for the orders to 'go', sometimes for as long as a week. The author of the ORB writes: 'It is not advisable to have them standing by for such a long period as a week as it is inclined to create 'jitters'.'

Despite the pressures of squadron life, Christmas was a comparatively happy affair. Losses had been light for the month, with only one crew – the crew of Flying Officer Derek Skinner DFC – being reported missing. It was initially hoped that they had survived after an aircraft was spotted in the Salt Marshes a few weeks later, but it proved to be a false dawn. The body of Skinner's rear gunner was washed ashore on the coast of Africa two months later, suggesting that the aircraft had come down in the sea. All were subsequently reported killed.[7]

To counteract the loss, several squadron personnel had been recommended for gallantry awards, among them, Flying Officer Alec Cranswick and Flying Officer Neville Cowan who both earned the DFC. (Cowan was later mentioned in despatches for operations in Malaya in 1954.) There were also three DFM submissions for Francis Adams, Alfred Sudden and James Starky, the latter a Kiwi who had recently survived a serious crash as a result of sabotage.

At one of the Landing Grounds, local Arabs had contaminated the fuel supply with water. Therefore, both the engines on Starky's Wellington cut out shortly after take-off, and although he managed to effect a full glide angle crash-landing, two members of crew were killed outright and others seriously injured. Had he not managed to jettison the bomb load, none would have survived. Having been knocked out and injured himself, Starky nonetheless set off into the desert to find help, walking twelve miles over rough terrain until staggering into LG060 covered in blood. He then guided an ambulance to the crash site. (With the completion of his first tour he returned to the UK and was commissioned. He later flew with 115 Squadron, winning both the DFC and DSO for gallantry, including one epic trip in which he flew his crippled bomber home when two of the crew bailed out and two more lay seriously injured.)

Christmas day was spent following the usual RAF tradition, with the officers serving the airmen their Christmas dinner. A planned game of football between the officers and NCO aircrew had to be abandoned because of bad weather. There was some fun, however. The CO organised a competition to find the best decorated billet. First prize went to the Maintenance Flight who had converted their living quarters into an English Pub, complete with balloons and streamers.

Yet, the brief respite did not last. Twelve aircraft were detailed for operations on the night of 28 December, some to bomb Piraeus harbour, others to drop supplies on the mainland, including Wellington 8494 flown by Pilot Officer Crossley and crew. All of the aircraft returned safely, although the attack was far from successful. The year ended with another operation of a similar nature that also passed without incident.

A New Year dawned with the prospect of little improvement in conditions or morale. It was to have dramatic consequences.

*   *   *

The crew list for January 1942, confirmed John as being in the 'A' Flight crew of Pilot Officer Crossley, the full crew comprising: Crossley (pilot); Pilot Officer Hodges (second pilot); Pilot Officer Baron (Air Observer); Sergeant Moore (w/op); Sergeant Brennan (w/op front gunner); and Sergeant Hutchinson (rear gunner). Hodges, who had shared flying duties with William Craig at OTU, had followed John to Kabrit; Craig was also flying as second pilot to Sergeant Povey and still had John Mahood as his regular observer and Ralph in charge of the wireless. Other familiar faces from Harwell included Harold 'Mickey' Vertican, posted in from 70 Squadron. The 'A' Flight commander was Squadron Leader Baird, and the next most senior officer Flight Lieutenant Cracknell who had been posted in towards the end of December. Cracknell's opposite number in 'B' Flight was Flight Lieutenant Thomas Prickett, at the time deputy to Squadron Leader Abbott DFC.

John celebrated his twenty-first birthday on 5 January with little to cheer. There was not even a can of beer with which to make a toast. As if by way of celebration, the desert decided to throw up one of its famous sandstorms that lasted until the early afternoon:

Sandstorms were incredible things to experience. They seemed to blow up out of nowhere. The wind would pick up sharply, and then you could see a darkening cloud on the horizon, moving quickly towards you. When they hit, you were completely blinded. I read somewhere that they were like London smog but made up of grit. That describes them exactly. You could not see your hand in front of your face. The grit would sting your eyes, and the sand would get in your mouth and turn to paste. In fact the sand would get everywhere. In your eyes, your mouth, your food, your water, your clothes, your bedding. Flying was impossible of course and you spent hours afterwards clearing it away. The strongest storms would blow away your tent, and scratch your face like sandpaper.

The pace of operations was about to increase significantly, and with it the casualty rates.

The focus of squadron activity in that first week of January was the planning of operations to Crete and mainland Greece to drop supplies. Two different modes of supply were envisaged, both with their challenges. The distances that needed to be travelled, even using the advanced landing grounds, were considerable, especially given that some of the targets lay in the foothills of Mount Olympus. Not surprisingly, at least one of the Wellingtons had to turn back because of shortage of fuel. Icing was another problem, as was the mountainous terrain and the apparently simple task of finding the drop zone. Local resistance fighters were supposed to be on hand to provide signals from the ground but they were not always forthcoming. Supplies, including rolls of blankets, were packed into 500lb and 250lb containers. Although, the principal issue, was not one of weight but rather bulk.

The Crossley crew took off on the early afternoon of John's birthday, a small trail of dust in their wake as they headed for LG060, a trip of around two hours. Their bomb racks were loaded with eighteen 250lb containers. They were one of three aircraft operating that night to Crete. Arriving at the ALG without mishap, they spent the rest of the afternoon helping the groundcrews to refuel their aircraft (Wellington J5524), before receiving the briefest of final briefings prior to their departure for the island. It was to prove to be a frustrating night for the crew:

> *The flight out to Crete across a large tract of the Mediterranean and approaching from the southeast was long but uneventful, but when we arrived, the observer could not make out a signal from below. Baron was as certain as he could be that we were in the right place, and Crossley circled for some time in the hope that he*

might catch a glimpse of our allies below. Keeping a careful watch
on our fuel, the Wellington could not stay long before our pilot,
the aircraft and its cargo were obliged to return home.

Of the three aircraft involved in that night's operations only one returned with its duty successfully carried out, that of Flight Lieutenant Prickett. Squadron Leader Abbott's Wellington developed a glycol leak, and in the end did not even get off the ground. Crossley returned to Crete the following night to drop his supplies irrespective of the response from the ground. They eventually returned to Kabrit in the late afternoon of the seventh.

After their marathon of endurance flying, Crossley and his crew were taken off operations for a few days although the rest of the Squadron was busy. Flight Lieutenant Douglas Cracknell crashed his aircraft on returning from operations on the seventh having become lost and running out of fuel. He managed to return later, apparently none the worse for his experience. The same could not be said, however, for the rest of his crew who were all treated for shock.[8]

Worse was to follow when Pilot Officer Thomas Geary and his crew failed to return from operations to attack enemy transport at Buerat El Hsun. Squadron Leader Baird was one of two pilots who reported seeing an aircraft hit by fire from a flak ship and exploding with a terrific flash[9]. It was presumed that this was the Wellington of the 20-year-old pilot. Among the dead were three Canadian aircrew.

Perhaps an even greater tragedy was the loss of 28-year-old Squadron Leader Maurice Abbott DFC on 19 January. Abbott was an extremely capable pilot, and a much admired and popular flight commander. He had been briefed to attack the submarine base at Salamis in poor weather but nothing was heard from him or his crew after take–off. An Italian broadcast on 21 January 1942 stated that an aircraft had been shot down over Elevsis.[10]

Extremely bad icing conditions were experienced by nearly every aircraft operating that night; only one was reported as having found the target. The rest returned with their bomb loads intact. It was a severe blow to have lost such an experienced pilot and leader.

There was more bad news for the squadron when it was reported on 18 January that the crew of Sergeant Raymond Shears, missing for over two months after an ill-fated 'mail run', had been found dead in the desert. His was one of two crews missing from the same operation. Indeed the month seemed to be cursed; not only were there deaths in the air but also on the ground, one of the native workers being killed when he was hit driving his lorry into the path of a Wellington that had been obliged to crash land.

The operational crews were becoming tired. Crash landings, forced landings, engine failures, sickness and early returns were becoming the order of the day. Nerves already taught were being stretched to breaking point. Sergeant Hill, the second pilot in Sergeant Starky's crew, overshot his landing and ran into soft sand, damaging the front turret and starboard airscrew. It was another accident that could have been avoided, and probably reflected the exhausted state of the men. Bill Astell, still not recovered from the serious injuries sustained in the crash landing in November, proceeded to Kenya on three month's sick leave. Others, including an officer observer near the start of his mercurial career, Flying Officer George Mackie, was categorised as operationally tired.[11]

Something had to give. A powder keg had unwittingly been lit and was about to explode in spectacular fashion.

*   *   *

On 2 February, the AOC 205 Group, Air Commodore MacLean, arrived to personally interview the squadron disciplinary officer about an incident involving no fewer than forty-five NCOs who had been placed under open arrest. Apparently, there were yet more NCOs under close arrest, those that were considered the ringleaders – the most dangerous. Wing Commander Rainsford, scheduled to return home via one of the new Consolidated Liberator long-range bombers then arriving in the Middle East, was obliged to remain for the court martial. The whiff of mutiny was in the air.[12]

The conditions within the squadron (to which John earlier referred) played a large part in the events that followed. It was, perhaps, no one single reason that caused the revolt, but rather an on-going series of minor grievances and miscalculations of morale, especially among the more senior officers about their NCO aircrew colleagues. Not only was there an 'us and them' mentality between aircrew officers and NCOs – and the geographical and social 'distance' they endured – but there was also antipathy among regular, non-flying NCOs towards flying colleagues of equal rank. Ever since the Air Ministry introduced the rule that all aircrew were to be granted the minimum rank of sergeant, noses had been put firmly out of joint by regular, non-aircrew sergeants who may have had to strive for twenty years or more to attain their rank, only to see another achieve the same in a matter of months.

There was also the question of leadership. It was not easy for a bomber squadron commander to impose his personality on his men at the best of times, but it was especially difficult when a large proportion of the men for which he was responsible did not even live on the camp, and had no opportunity or occasion to socialise in the mess (NCOs and officers messed separately). It was further complicated by the peripatetic nature of operations, with crews not unusually being away for several days at ALGs dotted around the desert.

In his thankless task, perhaps Rainsford might have looked to his senior warrant officer for support, but it appears that it was this very same warrant officer – a regular air force man – who was at the heart of much of the unhappiness. He might have looked therefore to the experience of the station commander, Group Captain Joe Fall, who as a First World War veteran of some renown, must surely have had to deal with sensitive issues of morale before. Indeed, he had been praised by his squadron commander in the first war for his support and encouragement of junior officers. But again, rather than being part of the solution, Fall appeared to be part of the problem.[13]

Fall, a stickler for discipline, had apparently decided that the NCO aircrew needed smartening up. How he arrived at such a decision is difficult to comprehend. His acolyte, the much-despised warrant officer, took it upon himself to execute the group captain's orders with unnecessary zeal. Orders were pinned to the notice board that all aircrew were to report to the warrant officer's office at 13.00hrs. Many of the NCOs had been on operations the night before, and indeed some had only just returned that morning and should have been excused any such duty.

With a mixture of irritation and bemusement they assembled to be told to draw rifles for a formal parade and rifle drill. At first, the NCOs obliged, until the ridiculousness of what they were being asked to do eventually dawned. It was certainly too much for one of their number, an Australian, who told the drill sergeant what he could do with his rifle, and threw it to the ground. This drew a furious reaction from the warrant officer in charge, who immediately ordered that the man be put under close arrest. This acted as a catalyst for others in the group to similarly throw down their rifles, and a near riot ensued.

The station adjutant was summoned and was faced with a dilemma. By rights, all of the men should have been placed under close arrest, but that meant they had to be escorted at all times by two others of equal or superior rank and that simply wasn't practical. He had to settle instead for placing the majority under open arrest while the principal culprits were dealt with.

John played no part in the mutiny, but had every sympathy for the conspirators:

> *I was aware of what was going on but was not directly involved. I had only been on the squadron for a few weeks by comparison to some of the others who had had to put up with poor conditions for six months or more with no end in sight.*
>
> *It is difficult to convey the boredom, the lack of anything meaningful or interesting to do. We had almost nothing, not even a newspaper to pass the time. Occasionally we had a visit from ENSA (Entertainments National Service Association) who put on a show but it wasn't enough. We used to be issued with fifty cigarettes a week and this was all very well but I didn't smoke. Some used to use them as stake money for gambling. They were called 'Cape to Cairo' though we nicknamed them 'Cough to Consumption'. They were apparently pretty rough.*

Not surprisingly, the 'mutiny' created considerable consternation at headquarters and retribution was swift. But it was not just the rebels themselves who were punished. Rainsford, who might have expected to have been awarded a Distinguished Service Order (DSO) at the end of his tour, was passed over for the honour, and Group Captain Fall returned to the UK soon after. It was perhaps fortunate that the revolt coincided with the arrival of a new commanding officer, and the opportunity for a new broom to sweep clean.

*   *   *

Squadron Leader (soon to be promoted wing commander) John Rollinson was a pre-war auxiliary officer who had been attached to 614 County of Glamorgan Squadron, an Army co-operation unit. An experienced pilot who learned to fly at his own expense, Rollinson was also a veteran of the desert war. The month before joining 148 Squadron he was awarded the DFC for his service with 38 Squadron on the recommendation of the AOC-in-C.

Operations throughout February followed the usual pattern and John was kept busy with a mixture of bombing and supply drops and sorties (from LG09) to Crete, Leros, and at least two 'mail runs' to Benghazi:

> *I cannot recall ever coming across an enemy fighter during a 'mail run' but the flak and searchlights could be intense and occasionally you could see lovely coloured lights snaking their way towards you or hear the rattle of shrapnel on the fuselage as one of the shells exploded a little too close for comfort. It was certainly not without risk.*
>
> *The way that Crossley and Baron behaved over the target was like watching a crew in a propaganda film of the time. The pilot would ask in that clipped voice: 'how are we doing navigator? I can't see a damn thing with all these searchlights'. Then, if he wasn't satisfied, he would call out 'dummy run' and we'd all have to go around and do it again. This of course was incredibly dangerous, and I don't believe I was the only one in the crew who just wanted the pair of them to drop the bombs and get home. Indeed, we used to discuss it when the officers weren't around. Crossley certainly wasn't lacking in courage, I would never say that, but I do think that the risk sometimes was greater than the reward.*

Another risk over the target came with the arrival of a new aircraft to the Middle East, the US-built Consolidated Liberator. The four-engined heavy bomber was designed to add further weight to the

Allied bombing attacks and was operated in very small numbers by 108 Squadron under the command of Wing Commander Richard Wells DFC and Bar.[14] Wells, a former flight commander with 148, flew the first RAF Liberator sortie in North Africa on the night of 10 January. It was an attack on the port of Tripoli and something of an experiment. Such was the initial promise, however, that the authorities accelerated plans for more aircraft to be delivered to the region, and staff officers from 205 Group sought to identify operationally tired crews who could act as ferry pilots. The difference in operational performance between the Liberator and the Wellington, however, led to practical difficulties:

> *On night operations in a Wellington, we would typically bomb from a height of around 8,000ft and sometimes lower, depending on the target and depending on the weight of bombs we were carrying. We were also somewhat limited in our range. The Liberator, however, could fly faster and further but more importantly, higher. Liberators would bomb from around 14,000ft and that meant two dangers; firstly, the flak would nearly always concentrate on the lower aircraft; and secondly, there was always the risk of being hit by bombs from above. Suffice to say not many of us liked to be on a raid at the same time as the Liberators.*

On the night of 9 February, the Crossley crew was one of only four of the twelve detailed for operations that successfully completed their sortie, and returned home, exhausted, after a seven-hour trip from the ALG. One of the other crews, captained by 'Mickey' Vertican, had a very lucky escape when the port engine of their Wellington blew up over the target area while on their bombing run. Vertican then battled for four hours to keep the Wellington in the air, nursing the one good engine to maintain height. Despite his efforts, the Wellington began to sink lower over the sea, until it was no more than 200ft above the wave tips, so low that they could see the white horses. The skipper then gave the order to ditch all unnecessary items that were not bolted down, including the guns and ammunition belts. Steadily, with their load lightened, they gained height to make landfall and crash land safe, but no doubt chastened by their experience. The ORB simply states: 'It is considered he put up a good show.'

The crew of Sergeant Hamilton failed to return from operations on the night of 23 February, a crew coming to the end of their first operational tour. Hamilton was on his forty-third trip and due to be rested; his wireless operator had already completed fifty. Both survived as prisoners of war. On that same day another squadron stalwart, Flying Officer Wisdom, crashed into a 55 Squadron Blenheim in a taxying incident. It appears that neither Wisdom, nor the ground crew who was guiding him, spotted the stationary bomber in time. Happily, no-one was injured. For Wisdom, however, it was a brief respite; he failed to return from operations five days later, his aircraft later reported as having been shot down in flames over Benghazi from a height of 3,000ft. The squadron received news on 24 March that Wisdom and his entire crew had survived and been taken prisoner.

*   *   *

The morning of 2 March was like any other; a typical day:

I reported to the crew room to discover that we were required for operations later in the day although the target was not yet known. We'd flown quite a few operations in February and some of the crew were clearly a little tired. 'Jock' had done more than most and had actually been identified as one of those due for a rest.

I took myself over to our aircraft to do what I did before every operation, which was to check over my guns. This meant removing them from the turret, stripping them down and giving them a thorough oil and a clean. First I had to peel away the condoms that I placed over the end of the barrels. The sand, as you can imagine, would find its way into every crevice and it was important that the guns were protected from the risk of 'jamming'. I would also very carefully check through the ammunition belt and examine each round and brush the cartridges until every grain of sand had been removed. Flight Lieutenant Woodley, our gunnery leader, impressed upon us that it didn't pay to take chances, and much as I trusted our excellent and diligent ground crew, I trusted myself more.[15]

Cleaning his guns took most of the morning with the Brownings broken down and parts laid out on a trestle table under canvas, and in the early afternoon John returned to the crew room with the rest of his crew and then assembled for the briefing. 'A' Flight was putting up six aircraft to leave at c14.00hrs to fly to LG09 and thence on to either Benghazi or Crete. Crossley, along with his flight commander, had been briefed for Crete, another supply-drop to partisans and Allied troops who had been left behind after the evacuation, and who were hiding out in the hills and carrying out a guerrilla war. The operation should have been completed two nights earlier but had been abandoned:

We were detailed to drop supplies to resistance fighters and our troops who had been left behind in Crete and who were living high in the mountains.

The aircraft we were allocated was an old Wellington, which used to have a mid-under gun turret known as a 'dustbin'. Because of the impact this 'dustbin' had on the aircraft's performance, it was only lowered when it was needed. Not surprisingly, the experiment didn't last very long and the device was removed and a cover fitted over the hole.

We were loaded up at Kabrit with blankets, clothing, bedding, medical supplies and food and flew to LG09 where we had to be patient and wait for the all clear for take-off. When we finally received permission to go, we arrived at the dropping zone without any problem but could not make out any indicator flares, a common problem. Knowing how precious our cargo was, and not wanting to see it drop into enemy hands, we circled for a good half hour before a shortage of fuel obliged us to return to base. It was an incredibly frustrating night. We had taken all the risk for little or no reward.

We got the all clear to go again the next night. Flying conditions were far from ideal. There was cloud up to around 10,000ft, and you could clearly see an electric storm brewing on the horizon. Visibility over the target area was once again very poor,[16] and Crossley had to battle with icing that slowed our progress and made the Wellington all but 'hang' in the air.

Despite these conditions, we managed to make a successful landfall over the coast of the island before the problems really started. One of our engines, which must have been running rough for a little while or couldn't cope with the extra strain being placed upon it in the cloud, suddenly caught fire. It was not a happy sight.

Crossley didn't panic. Both the engines had a fire suppression system built into the engine covers, which could be activated by pressing a button within the cockpit. The pilot did just that and waited anxiously for the extinguisher to take effect. Within a few moments, a roaring fire with flames stretching back to the tailplane had been reduced to little more than a smoulder, with sparks and black smoke suggesting that all was still not quite right. A calamity had been averted, but the danger had not yet passed.

With the engine now effectively useless, the pilot 'feathered' the propeller; this prevented the blades from rotating and thereby caused a drag on the aircraft. A Wellington could fly on one engine but not for long, and certainly not if there was other damage. It could not maintain the same height and its speed would be drastically reduced. John realised they were in for a difficult and uncomfortable flight home, with a large stretch of water to navigate before they could reach the safety of dry land. LG09 was still some four hundred miles distant:

> *We slowly started to lose height, and had no alternative but to abandon our operation and set course for base. The pilot instructed me to start jettisoning all loose equipment. I climbed out of my turret and made my way aft. I started with the blankets and other items such as medical supplies, clothing, etc, that were bundled inside the aircraft. The pilot already jettisoned the supplies that were stored in the bomb bays.*
>
> *I next got rid of my own guns and ammunition and then helped 'Jock' with his, throwing them out of the open hatch, and followed by the oxygen bottles and anything else I could find that I thought we didn't need, such as the Elsan toilet that I hacked free using the emergency axe. Then that went overboard along with the extinguishers. Finally I turned to our own items of personal gear, our flying clothing and even our parachutes. I must have been pretty confident that our skipper would get us home!*

Despite John's best efforts, the Wellington continued to lose height until the second engine spluttered and died and it became inevitable that they would have to ditch:

I was already prepared for this. The skipper ordered us to take up crash positions I removed the astrodome, which was one of my responsibilities, and took my place by the bed, half way down the fuselage. I lay on the bed with my hands behind my head and feet on the main spar and waited for the impact.

Ditching an aircraft in water was a hazardous exercise, even in perfect conditions with all engines and control functions operating fully. It was substantially more difficult for aircraft whose balance and control were impacted by two dud engines. Crossley knew the form; he knew to aim the aircraft to come down along the line of the waves, rather than across them. He also knew to take off as much speed as he could before hitting the water, for the chances of cartwheeling and finally breaking an already damaged aircraft were high. With considerable skill, Crossley managed to keep the nose up and the wings level as they skidded across the top of the waves:

When we hit the water, the noise was intense, a loud scraping sound as though the bottom of the aircraft was being sliced open. It seemed to last an eternity before it finally stopped and the aircraft slew to one side as the water washed over the wings. Actually the landing had been remarkably smooth, all things considered.

We all knew that a heavy bomber could sink within seconds and there were other dangers. We'd heard stories of aircrew being caught in trailing aerials and dragged down with their aircraft, but to be honest the only thing that crossed my mind at the time was making it into the dinghy as quickly as possible.

The dinghy was designed to inflate on contact with water and it was already reassuringly bobbing up and down in the swell, attached to the wing of the Wellington by a sturdy cord. I made a dive for it and missed! Fortunately, I was still able to clamber on board and immediately started baling since the dinghy was already half full with water.

I was exhausted from the effort, but still had enough energy to help the others climb on board which they did with considerable effort. As we sat in the dinghy, congratulating ourselves on our lucky escape and grateful for the skill of our pilot, we realised that the dinghy was still attached to the aircraft and the Wellington was beginning to sink!

The skipper asked if anyone had a penknife and fortunately the wireless operator had one. He had just managed to cut the long cord when there was a strange gurgling noise and the aircraft slipped beneath the sea and disappeared. A few seconds later and we could have been in real trouble.

John and his colleagues were soaked to the skin but safe. They were dressed only in their tropical gear – shirts and shorts with an inflatable Mae West. The water temperature at that time of year was still around fifteen degrees centigrade, and to that end they were lucky. (By comparison the temperature of the North Sea at that time of year was nearer six degrees.) The wireless operator had sent out a distress call and clamped down the morse key to fix their position. John had a quick look about the dinghy and noticed that the emergency supplies – including drinking water and malt-tablets – were missing. All that was left was a paddle and a heliograph for signalling.

It was still dark, and the crew could see the lights of various coastal vessels twinkling tantalisingly in the gloom but always, it seemed, just out of reach. They were only four miles or so off the coast at Daba. Frustratingly close. They watched the dawn slowly arrive and the sun lift reassuringly over the horizon; with the warmth of the sun's rays their hopes began to rise. Although the ships were many miles away, the captain made them wave their life preservers and shout 'Ship ahoy' to draw their attention. It might have been funny in different circumstances.

After four hours of drifting, their throats dry and their voices hoarse from shouting, they heard the faint throbbing of an aero engine somewhere in the sky. Then the sound became louder, and the familiar and friendly shape of Wellington came into view; it was one of the dedicated Sea Rescue Flight[17] that had been formed at Kabrit the previous year. The aircraft circled the men in their life raft several times before swooping in close to drop a brightly coloured marker buoy that landed with a splash just a few hundred feet from the dinghy. With a waggle of its wings the aircraft then sped away, radio-ing as it did so, for a high-speed rescue launch to come to their aid. A few hours later they were safe in Alexandria.

They arrived back at Kabrit by train on the evening of 3 March. Earlier in the day the base had been raided by enemy aircraft which had dropped delayed action and incendiary bombs, destroying two of the Squadron's Wellingtons and damaging three others. Ground crews and pioneer corps troops were still filling in the craters gouged from the runway when they arrived back to be interviewed by the Group Intelligence Officer, Squadron Leader Bartlett, and his fellow IO, Flight Lieutenant Brown.

Both agreed that Crossley had pulled off a textbook ditching.

Chapter 4

On Dry Land

Although the crew were in the mood to celebrate, the ditching had in fact taken its toll. Nerves were frayed. John knew they had pushed their luck. They had been lucky, not only in surviving being brought down over the sea, but also in making contact with friendly forces:

> *Communications equipment in the Middle East at that time was very poor. We only had high frequency radios and their range was limited. Our navigators had none of the sophisticated electronic equipment that was available later in the war; they had to navigate using the stars, dead reckoning, and the occasional visual reference, if anything could be seen in the moonlight. Had we not made it so close to the coast, we might never have been found, or been found by our enemy and spent the rest of the war 'in the bag'. In the worst case we may have crashed and never been discovered until our bodies were washed up on a beach some weeks later.*

The five men were debriefed on their return and found that they were not the only ones to have had an eventful evening. Squadron Leader Baird had the unnerving experience of passing a Heinkel III on his return, North of Alexandria, skulking back from a raid on Kabrit! Upon landing he ran over an unexploded bomb that fortunately didn't go off, and probably considered he'd had a lucky escape.

The Crossley crew were given an immediate seven-day 'survivors leave'. John spent his in the tranquillity of Tel Aviv, journeyed to by train with Dougie and Jock. Within a few short months the three of them had become firm friends. Dougie, from Brighton was full of energy; 'Jock', from Edinburgh, was more contained:

> *Dougie was quite a boy, always full of beans. 'Jock' was considerably quieter, a short, little man who rarely spoke, but when he did he started every sentence with a long 'ermmm…' that we used to mimic.*
>
> *We had been in Tel Aviv no more than a few hours when we came across a party of half a dozen or so Australian soldiers. They were perhaps a little the worse for wear and seemed to have a beef with us that some of their troops had been bombed by the RAF, or that we weren't there when they needed us. I'm not sure now and I'm not sure they knew or cared at the time, I just think they were letting off steam. Anyway it all kicked off, quite a few punches were thrown and we ended up fleeing for our lives. So much for our Allies!*

The three NCOs enjoyed their brief flirtation with peace, relaxing on the beach during the day and drinking freshly squeezed Jaffa orange juice to keep them cool. Their accommodation in a beachside hotel was basic but welcome, and all three slept for great passages of time, the strain and fatigue of operations at last beginning to show.

All too soon their leave was over and they returned to the Squadron to find that one of the Australian pilots, Pilot Officer Jeffrey Pelletier and his crew from 'B' Flight had gone missing on the night of 7 March. They too had the good fortune of coming down in the sea, taking to their dinghy, and being rescued twelve hours later by a launch having been spotted by a Walrus (a small amphibious reconnaissance aircraft built by Supermarine) of the Fleet Air Arm. They returned to the Squadron soon after fit and well, with the exception of the second pilot (Alan Black RNZAF) who had a broken collar bone. He had been hit with an anchor thrown by one of the Walrus crew!

John was briefed for operations for the evening of 13 March, one of five 'A' Flight aircraft operating that night. Flying from Kabrit in the early afternoon they were detailed for special operations over Greece but were obliged to return when their Wellington (K – 8494) developed engine trouble over the target, obliging Crossley to shut it down.

A sense of déjà vu pervaded the mood in the aircraft. Flying a Wellington on one engine over sea and desert was not a cheerful prospect. The observer had to use all of his navigational skills to guide his pilot home. History, however, was not to repeat itself and they returned safely to the ALG, landing a little after five thirty in the morning. It had been an epic flight of more than 450 miles, and the landing had to be made in the dark.

They were taken off operations the following day.

*   *   *

The squadron commander and his medical officer had realised that Crossley and his crew needed to be taken out of the front line, and out of harm's way, albeit temporarily. Lance Baron, the observer, reported sick (though he would soon recover and take on the role as squadron navigation officer) while Crossley was himself posted to LG106 to assume duties as Officer i/c Operations to assist Flying Officer Harry 'Tex' Hambleton (a colourful character, Hambleton was later awarded the MBE for his services with 148 Squadron). John went with him:

After our ditching, and the return from survivors' leave, we were sent to the landing ground near El Daba about 180 km to

the west of Alexandria, primarily to help carry out repair and
maintenance work, and ensure the landing ground continued to
be ready for operations when needed.

The conditions were very basic and exposed. Although the
days were very hot, the evenings conversely were bitterly cold,
and we were accommodated under canvas (Crossley shared with
one of the Intelligence Officers, Flying Officer Roy Chappell,
with whom he had struck up a particularly close friendship.)

On each side of the landing strip there were numerous mounds
of compacted sand that presented a hazard to any aircraft at
take-off and landing, especially at night or in poor visibility.
There was an army camp nearby and the soldiers gave us a hand
in levelling them off. They also helped us to dig quite a sizeable
trench (it was well over 6ft deep and 6ft across) that we could use
as a Flying Control.

The troops, who were from the Pioneer Corps, were kept busy. As
well as the Flying Control bunker, they also dug trenches to create a
Briefing Room and serve as the Intelligence headquarters. A 'dummy'
site was also constructed, with the purpose of deceiving future enemy
raiders who had become a growing nuisance. The digging, however,
and the movement of tents and provisions had several unintended
consequences. Not least it provoked the local wildlife; snakes and
scorpions that had found solace in the shade were not best pleased at
being disturbed, and Crossley was himself on the receiving end of a
painful scorpion's sting.

John had been at the landing ground less than a week when an
incident reminded the men of the dangers on the ground as well as in
the air, especially when it came to manhandling several tons of bombs,
ammunition and fuel. It also showed the value of digging trenches.

Seventeen crews (nine from 148 and eight from 104 Squadrons) were in the Briefing Room when an airman rushed in shouting that 'T' Tommy – a 104 Squadron aircraft – was on fire. As the aircrew emerged, they saw a Wellington was already well ablaze and so promptly took cover. They needed no second bidding. A fire tender bravely attempted to douse the flames, but its crew was beaten back by the intense heat and the unequal battle. Now it was simply a question of waiting until the bomb load went up, which it subsequently did with an almighty 'whoomph'. Shrapnel and debris from the shattered aircraft rose hundreds of feet into the sky and began to fall like miniature comets, complete with fiery tales, spreading further disruption and damage. But not panic; the men had seen it all before.

Rollinson, the 148 Squadron CO who was present at the time, took command of the situation. He ordered that none of the aircraft closest to 'Tommy' when she exploded would be allowed to operate that night, and all other aircraft also had to be inspected, irrespective of their place in the aerodrome. In the event, twelve of the seventeen were ultimately deemed 'safe', albeit that they took off much later than originally planned. The raid was not a success, severe electrical storms and icing completing a thoroughly miserable day.

Blame for the accident rested at the feet of the crew. They had been making adjustments to the flare fuses and turning the fuse-setting ring when one of them ignited, causing a chain reaction of spectacular proportions. It was a miracle that nobody was killed. In the morning, only the tail of the stricken bomber survived, standing tall and erect as though creating its own tombstone.

March, a month in which so much had happened, concluded badly. Half a dozen aircraft took off from LG106 in the late evening of 27 March for a 'mail run' and two failed to return: Sergeant 'Jimmy' Wild was reported 'missing'; Flight Sergeant Edward Papworth was reported to have crashed at Mersa Matruh. As it happened, Papworth was the only fatality. He had completed the bombing of Benghazi successfully and had handed over control of the aircraft to his second pilot, Sergeant Donald Moon[1]. All seemed well until the engines began to surge when they were only forty miles from home, and Moon attempted to synchronise them. Perhaps distracted, both by their need to stabilise the aircraft and a flashing beacon ahead, he failed to take into account their height until the Wellington literally bounced in. The surface of the ground was such that the aircraft was badly damaged, and the 21-year-old-captain killed.

'Jimmy' Wild had rather better luck. No sooner had he dropped his bombs than the aircraft was hit by flak, causing what proved to be fatal damage. The Wellington steadily lost height over a period of forty minutes, with the captain battling the controls, before he finally had to give in to the inevitable, crashing into the side of a hill, a few miles east of Tolmeta in Cyrenaica. Apart from the rear gunner, who was knocked unconscious and had a broken nose, the rest emerged remarkably unscathed.

Wild and his crew took stock of their predicament while they waited for their rear gunner to recover. They gathered what provisions they could from inside of the aircraft including the dinghy's emergency rations, half a gallon of water, three tins of bully beef and two cartons of chocolate, and set off for home.

The going was hard and they covered little more than seven miles on the first day. On the second day they reached the Barce/Cyrene border and crossed it under cover of darkness. They continued on their journey, keeping the road in sight to aid with navigation, but had a scare on the fourth night when they found themselves surrounded by German soldiers. For a brief moment they thought they would be captured, but the moment passed and they were taken in hand by a friendly Senussi tribesman who gave them food. They again narrowly missed being captured by an enemy patrol and were obliged to cross an Italian minefield to escape. On the twelfth day they were found by soldiers of the Long Range Desert Group and led to safety. They arrived back at the landing ground bearded, bedraggled, but otherwise none the worse for their experiences. They became proud members of the late arrivals club, the 'flying boot', awarded to all aircrew that managed to make it home on foot (or other means) having been shot down in the desert. They were also all later mentioned in despatches.[2]

The pace of operations increased in April as did the frustration of the officer commanding 148 Squadron. Rollinson wrote to the AOC 205 Group at the start of the month with regards the effectiveness of the bombing of Benghazi harbour. The squadron had been tasked with bombing specific landing stages but the chances of hitting such pinpoint targets, in the wing commander's opinion, from 12,000ft and in the teeth of fierce enemy opposition, were few and far between. The standard of training, he argued, was simply not up to it, and the number of bombs they were able to carry did not allow for a wide enough spread. Rollinson's view was that the squadron would be better employed attacking targets such as ammunition dumps and munition stores, where the results were more tangible and immediate.

Rollinson certainly had a point, and his thoughts reflected the frustrations of his men. The 'targets' were primarily a series of 'moles' and wrecks within the harbour that were used for unloading supplies. The moles included 'central' and 'cathedral'; the wrecks had been filled with concrete to become artificial 'piers' and were given codenames such as Johnny, Harry and George. They had once rejoiced in more romantic names including Maria Eugenia and Gloriastella, but now served a very different purpose. While the official reports recorded considerable success against the land-based targets (the port facilities, railway lines and warehouses), the wrecks had emerged virtually unscathed.

In the meantime, the Squadron stuck to its task, now in the throes of relocating from Kabrit to LG106 on a more permanent basis. Sergeant Nethercote and his crew went missing on the night of 6 April having force landed 130 miles east of Benghazi with only one engine working. After several adventures and near misses, they were eventually picked up safe and well by a Free French patrol. Such was the fluidity of the desert war, and the limited number of bomber aircraft available, that a detachment of ten aircraft and seventeen crews from 148 Squadron left for Malta in the middle of the month to commence operations against targets in Sicily:

> *We were left behind, perhaps fortunately so, for our colleagues arrived to a metaphorical and literal baptism of fire, two of their aircraft being destroyed in a heavy bombing raid soon after landing at Luqa. What was doubly frustrating for them and us was that the aircraft lost were both 'Peggies' – Wellington 1Cs with Pegasus engines. The experiment with the Merlin-engined aircraft had been largely a failure, and throughout the month the Squadron's aircraft and spares were brought up to strength based on the more reliable Pegasus-engined variant. The Merlin aircraft and their engines soon disappeared.*[3]

The squadron's detachment to Luqa, although short-lived, was not an especially happy one. As well as losing several aircraft on the ground, they also lost two highly experienced crews on the night of 23 April. The target was Comiso. Opposition was heavy, with flak accounting for the Wellingtons of 29-year-old Australian Flying Officer Roderick Harper, and a 21-year-old Englishman from Berkshire, Flight Lieutenant Tony Hayter.

Hayter had learned to fly before the war and flew his first Strategic Reconnaissance sortie with 57 Squadron in France in May 1940. It was almost his last, landing back at base with more than 200 bullet holes in his Blenheim, having been intercepted by no fewer than three Bf109s. Hayter had indeed led something of a charmed life, and was mentioned in despatches for flying a British army officer to Merryville to impart plans for the evacuation of Dunkirk. Converting to Wellingtons he flew bomber operations in Western Europe before being posted to the Middle East and arriving at 148 Squadron in January 1942. He had already survived a crash landing in the desert before being shot down over Comiso on the southern tip of Sicily. But his luck finally ran out two years later as a prisoner of war when, as one of 'The Fifty', he was murdered by the Gestapo for his part in the Great Escape.

The month was not an entire wash out. On the thirteenth, Jock was recommended for the DFM, giving John and Dougie much cause for celebration. Even the skipper, Don Crossley, extended his congratulations to the quiet Scot.

The citation for Jock's DFM credited him with dozens of operations as front gunner in attacks on targets in Germany, Greece, Crete, Sicily, and Cyrenaica. It noted his 'great keenness for operational flying' and his 'disregard for danger', both of which, it said, 'have set an inspiring example to all aircrews of the squadron and particularly to inexperienced crews joining the unit'.

Rollinson returned from Malta on the twenty-eighth to add his congratulations before departing for a well-earned leave.

*   *   *

The monotony of operations continued throughout the weeks ahead, the Squadron's brief and regrettable sojourn to the historic island of Malta quickly forgotten as the 'mail run' once again became the order of the day. The AOC seemed almost obsessed: RAF bombers attacked Benghazi on twenty-three nights in March, twenty-four in April, and twenty-one in May. While other targets in Greece and in the desert itself were occasionally paid a visit, Benghazi remained at the top of the list.

Despite operating the more reliable Wellington 1Cs, engines that had been flogged for hundreds of miles in extreme temperatures were still prone to fail, and small numbers of aircraft would frequently return early or fail to get off the ground in the first place.

In preparation for a planned Allied military offensive, and to seize the initiative from the Afrika Korps, the Squadron moved almost all of its crews and ground crew echelons to the advanced landing ground in the second and third weeks of May, and therefore closer to the front line. Large convoys of trucks and an even larger degree of logistical nous were needed to ship the equipment and supplies required to sustain an operational squadron.

As it happened, it was the Germans and their exceptional leader, Erwin Rommel, who struck first, opening a new offensive on 26 May with a feint that masked the real thrust towards Bir Hakeim, an area held by the Free French. The attack coincided with the arrival of a new Squadron CO, Wing Commander Douglas Kerr, who assumed command on the twenty-ninth. Kerr, who was only 25 and an old-Cranwellian, arrived wearing the purple and crimson ribbon of the Distinguished Service Order (DSO) that he had been awarded as a squadron leader with 70 Squadron. He demanded a maximum effort from the veterans of 148 Squadron, and he got it.

That night, fifteen crews took off to attack landing ground targets in Tmimi, about seventy miles to the west of Tobruk, a port once again under threat from the advancing Axis troops. Two Wellingtons failed to return, one each from 'A' and 'B' Flights: 21-year-old Flying Officer James Brown force landed following an engine failure, apparently though lack of oil. After setting fire to their aircraft, the crew walked for eight hours to the frontier wire of El Beida, making contact with a Bristol Bombay, an air transport workhorse, that had no doubt been sent out to look for them and which dropped water, supplies and a message that help was on its way at the second time of asking. A Military police vehicle was despatched to pick them up.

Flight Lieutenant Jack Watts was similarly forced down as a result of high oil temperature. At the time he was at 6,500ft photographing the target when the engine started to vibrate violently and then packed up, and he eventually belly-landed three miles north of Bir Hakeim. With the sound of battle ringing in their ears, the crew also set light to their bomber and destroyed anything of potential intelligence value to the enemy – including eating the 'flimsies', the thin pieces of paper on which the codes or frequencies of the day may be written.[4] Skirting a minefield and what they took to be an enemy camp, they came under fire from machine guns and rifles, obliging them to stand up and surrender. They were relieved to see the opposition wearing British Army tin hats and were identified as Free French. With much back-slapping and hand shaking all round, the crew was safe, but only temporarily so.

The strongpoint, it appeared, was cut off and under constant attack, and Watts had to persuade a party of Kings Royal Rifles to take them through the lines. They had to dodge another minefield and a small force of Italian soldiers before finally making it to the headquarters of 7th Armoured Division. After a good meal and every courtesy, they were escorted to Gambut and handed over to the RAF. (In his subsequent report, Watts states that the Army definitely believed that 'the lack of enemy air activity over the Battle Front is due to the good services rendered by the RAF.' This is an interesting contrast against the belief of the Army during the evacuation at Dunkirk two years earlier that the RAF had all-but deserted them.)

Further losses were recorded two nights later when the Wellingtons of Flying Officer Astell and Sergeant Rees failed to return. Rees turned up safe, having crash landed at LG05 after being badly shot up and with a splinter wound in his shoulder. Of Bill Astell there was no immediate word. Only when he arrived back to his unit several days later did the full story emerge of yet another close shave.

Astell had been ordered to bomb the airfield at Birbet El Chieba and was circling the airfield at 3,000ft when he had the shock of seeing tracer rounds enter and pass through his starboard wing. They had not seen their assailant, a single engine night fighter, before it was too late and the damage was terminal. The hydraulics were shot up and a fire quickly took hold in the fuselage. The navigator jettisoned the balance of their bombs and Astell took stock. As he was doing so, the fighter came in for a second pass, setting the starboard wing on fire and hitting both the wireless operator, who was manning one of the beam guns, in the leg and the second pilot in the arm.

The captain ordered his crew to bail out, but only three of the crew managed to do so with sufficient height to land safely. (The wounded second pilot had to be helped into his parachute.) Bill Astell and his navigator were obliged to stay with the aircraft, which now resembled a flaming torch, and crash land close to one of the landing grounds that they had just bombed. Both men had a grandstand view of the Wellington's handiwork as they set out, somewhat dazed and in shock but otherwise in one piece, to put as much distance between them and their blazing aircraft as possible before the enemy arrived.

After a second night of walking, the two were exhausted and had drunk what little water they had managed to salvage from the wreck. They passed close to a German flak emplacement, where they found the soldiers asleep. With remarkable temerity, they managed to filch an onion, a pair of socks and a tin of red peppers while the troops continued to snore loudly! Continuing into the night, they stumbled into a Wadi and filled their water bottles from a German water container that was found conveniently by a tent with four men inside. Again they managed to make off without being detected, and found a bush in which to hide as dawn broke; they found themselves in what seemed to be the middle of a camp comprising a variety of soft-skinned and tracked vehicles. Waiting for night to fall, they refilled their water bottles and crept away, heading east. The next twenty-four hours followed a similar pattern, laying up during the day and walking by night. Now effectively in the middle of two opposing armies, they were shelled by both Allied and Axis artillery the following day, later discovering that their place of refuge was in fact an Observation Post (OP) well favoured by both sides!

The two men played a deadly game of hide and seek with the enemy forces, sometimes being so close as to hear them talking, the distinctive guttural sound of German drifting in the night air. The physical and mental strain, however, was beginning to take its toll, and Astell's navigator, Pilot Officer Alfred Whitfield 'Bishop' Dodds (Dodds was a former parson), was on the point of collapse. Spotting an armoured car, and hoping it to be British, Astell left his friend under cover and pushed on to make contact. Drained of energy, the pilot was not able to do so, and when he returned to where he thought he had left his navigator, he couldn't find him. He searched frantically for well over an hour before having to admit defeat. Now on the verge of collapse himself, he summoned sufficient strength to work his way along a wire fence that he believed led to the Allied positions. He was in luck. As he entered into yet another Wadi he was challenged by a soldier of the Rand Light Infantry and after proving his identity, was taken to meet the Regiment's CO, Lieutenant Colonel Thomas. Astell acquainted Thomas with his predicament, and the officer despatched a patrol to search for Dodds but without success.[5]

At Base they too came under attack, despite the OC's request for more ground defences, and the nights were now typically punctuated by the crunch of bombs exploding close by, or the drone of aircraft engines overhead. Crossley received a well-deserved Distinguished

Flying Cross, the second of the crew to receive an award for gallantry. New crews were posted in to replace those that had been lost or were now tour-expired, and the more experienced men helped bring them up to speed with local flying conditions.

These losses never really affected me. Perhaps they should have done, but I was somehow immune to it. Isolated perhaps. When a crew went missing, it was expected. It was a risk we took and nobody complained about it, or if they did, then no-one listened. Even when the commanding officer went missing it made no difference.

What was always surprising was when a crew that you had thought was lost later turned up alive and well. Some have suggested that these operations in the Middle East carried less risk than operations over Europe. In Europe, they faced danger from flak and fighters from the moment they crossed into enemy territory. In the desert, it is true, we only had to contend with the defences over the target, but we also had to face a greater danger and that was the desert itself.

If you were hit or suffered an engine failure, you faced a flight of many hundreds of miles across a barren wasteland with little or no hope of salvation if you came down. If you crashed or bailed out, without water you could be dead within days. Those who made it back, therefore, were something of a miracle to us; something to be marvelled at. To give you hope. They would wander into camp unannounced, their faces and lips scorched by the sun, their hair unkempt and the first signs of a beard appearing on their chins, looking like spectres at a feast.

On the ground, the Germans made swift advances, but were for a time thwarted by the heroic actions of the Free French under the command of the ironically named General Koenig. Rommel skirted around the stubborn Frenchmen, and pressed the British, capturing the headquarters of 7th Armoured Division. A fierce tank battle on 13 and 14 June obliged the Allied troops into a tactical withdrawal to more prepared positions at El Alamein. Tobruk fell by the evening of 20 June with the capture of 30,000 men and a large amount of stores and equipment.

A difficult situation for the British was fast becoming critical, evidenced by the action of the British Commander, General Auchinleck, in relieving his subordinate General Ritchie of his command and assuming responsibility himself for holding the line. (Auchinleck would himself be replaced only a few weeks later by General 'Hap' Alexander while command of the Eighth Army passed to the mercurial talent of General Montgomery.)

> *The squadron operated on every night that the weather allowed, striking the German supply routes at the rear as well as maintaining attacks on Greece and in particular the port of Piraeus. The Germans, in turn, strengthened their own defences; there was a marked increase in the number of heavy guns now firing at us over Benghazi. The 'mail run' had lost none of its intensity or danger.*

Perhaps inevitably, losses began to mount.

Flight Lieutenant Vincent Gane and his crew went missing on the night of 7 June. Gane had been posted to the Squadron from the Sea Rescue Flight, and was an experienced pilot. On the night in question, he had successfully dropped his bombs on the target and flown out to sea to observe the results, when his starboard engine began to misbehave. The oil pressure dropped as the temperature rose alarmingly. To stop it from seizing altogether, Gane switched it off to cool it down, but had to sacrifice height to do so. As such he followed the now tried and tested formula of relieving the Wellington of any excess weight, guns, ammunition belts and other paraphernalia falling into the sea below.

Gane's attempts to keep the aircraft in the air were thwarted when the temperature in the port engine also began to rise, to the point that he was obliged to crash land, the engine bursting into flames as he did so. The crew survived and took stock of their situation and their resources, gathering water and maps and what rations they could find before heading off in a vaguely easterly direction. The intense heat made the going painfully slow, and the men were forced into taking frequent stops.

For almost three days the men stumbled through the desert until eventually, the skipper and his navigator were the only two fit enough to push on ahead to the frontier wire. Dodging enemy patrols, they had the good fortune to see the pudgy shape of a twin-engined Baltimore above them, and sent up a flare. The pilot of the Baltimore spotted the red Very light rising up into the sky and circled for ten minutes like a mechanical bird of prey to pinpoint its source before flying off, satisfied by what he had seen. By now, the remainder of the crew had caught up, and the five men rested to await developments. Their patience was rewarded later that same afternoon when two more friendly aircraft (a Martin Maryland and Lysander[6]) appeared, and at some risk landed close by. The men, re-vitalised by the sight of their rescuers, and the water and beer they had brought with them, were quick to clamber on board, and were soon on their way to freedom.

Gane was none the worse for his adventure and made several recommendations based on his experience, including a note to include Vaseline and soap in future first aid kits to help with blisters. His wireless operator, however, was in a bad way, having been severely affected by a combination of dehydration, exhaustion and shock. (Gane would later return to the UK and fly operations with 103 Squadron in the winter of 1944, being awarded the DFC as an acting squadron leader.)

While the flight lieutenant and his crew were still unaccounted for in the desert, another of the squadron's crews had a lucky escape. On 9 June, Pilot Officer Albert Loos, a relative newcomer to the squadron, took off as one of six aircraft to bomb the airfield at Heraklion on Crete. On the return flight his port engine failed and he was alarmed to see the propeller spinning off into the night, luckily without causing any damage to the mounting or the fuselage. He diverted to LG14 and landed without further incident but chastened by his experience. (Loos was awarded the DFC in January 1943.)

Engine problems were once again occurring with monotonous, and potentially fatal, regularity. Fuel and oil consumption were also an issue, leading captains to distrust the serviceability of their aircraft, notwithstanding the heroic efforts of the ground crews. The weather also played its part, a ground fog being directly responsible for an accident on the night of 15 June when one of the Canadian NCO pilots, Sergeant William Ross, misjudged his height coming into land and crashed heavily. The crew scrambled clear, much shaken, before the aircraft caught fire and soon after exploded. (Ross was awarded the DFC having been commissioned in February 1943. By that time he had completed forty-one operations, including fourteen raids on Tobruk. He was later shot down and made prisoner in July 1943 while flying with 428 Squadron.)

The crash led to the second pilot, Sergeant R. G. Gravell, being deemed unfit for future operations, his nerve seemingly gone. Another more senior pilot, Jack Watts, who had only recently survived an ordeal over Tmimi and shared his experiences with his fellow aircrew, also expressed his mistrust in the Pegasus XVIII engines and refused to fly. Morale was at low ebb. NCOs and commissioned men did not mind risking their lives to enemy action, but were damned if they were going to be sent into battle with a weapon they could not trust.

The CO, understandably, was not best pleased with us, and assembled the men in a formal parade to give us all a dressing down. To be asked to be taken off operations, he argued, showed the 'wrong spirit', and everyone should be prepared to 'stretch it a bit'. Some, however, had clearly already been stretched to breaking point, and although the gravity of their situation was well understood, exhausted men were a risk to themselves and their crews. We listened, but I'm not sure that anyone paid much attention.

Perhaps the nadir of the Squadron came on the night of 22 June. The target was Gazala, and Wing Commander Kerr was leading the way in Wellington ES990 with Pilot Officer Frederick Westcott in the second pilot's seat. The wingco was dropping flares and flying at around 4,000ft over the target, when other crews saw the aircraft hit by flak and burst into flames. It was as though the flak had deliberately concentrated on his Wellington and his Wellington alone. Kerr seemed to be in control of his aircraft as it descended a further 2,000ft before suddenly and dramatically diving into the ground and exploding. Perhaps the CO had been wounded; perhaps some vital control wires finally snapped. What was certain was that all of the men were killed – including the 19-year-old rear gunner – with the exception of Westcott who was thrown clear. In a strange quirk of fate that is virtually impossible to explain, he awoke to find himself alive, on the ground, with his parachute opened beside him. (Frederick Westcott, whose middle names were William Ashplant, survived and went on to have a distinguished post-war career, retiring as a group captain in 1977.)

Command of the Squadron passed temporarily to Thomas Prickett (by now a squadron leader) before the arrival of a permanent replacement the following day.

*   *   *

For some, the Middle East was the proving ground; many – like Cranswick and Astell – learned their trade in the scorching days and freezing nights of the desert and went on to perfect their skills in different theatres of war including Pathfinders; others arrived in North Africa with their credentials already firmly established. One of these was Wing Commander James Warne.

Warne, a 26-year-old Cornishman, exuded authority and confidence from the start, which was not surprising given his experience. A pre-war regular, Warne wore the faded ribbon of a DFC with a silver rosette to denote that it had been awarded twice (referred to as a 'Bar'), evidence of the first forays of bomber command over Western Europe in the winter of 1940–41. He had earned his first award flying the Armstrong Whitworth Whitley with 102 Squadron, and added the Bar with 58 Squadron twelve months later. He had survived his fair share of scrapes and near misses and had also suffered personal tragedy with the loss of his brother Paul in the early stages of the war, shot down in a Blenheim following an attack on Stavangar during the Norwegian campaign.

Despite his undoubted talents, Warne was unable to influence what happened on the ground, and the Eighth Army's battle with the Afrika Korps. The RAF, however, was well prepared for an organised retreat, a credit to the AOC-in-C, Air Marshal Arthur Tedder, his planning staff and his operational commanders. The landing grounds had been established along excellent lines of communication, and were well stocked with supplies of fuel, ammunition and bombs. It was a comparatively simple task for a squadron of aircraft and its men to withdraw from one base and begin operating from another in relative safety, almost immediately (notwithstanding the enormous logistical planning that lay behind it). It meant that the pace of operations against the enemy advance could be maintained, frustrating the Germans'

Confirmation Day. John is third from left, third row.

Angela and John before John's departure to the Middle East. Angela wears a sweetheart brooch; John an air gunner's brevet.

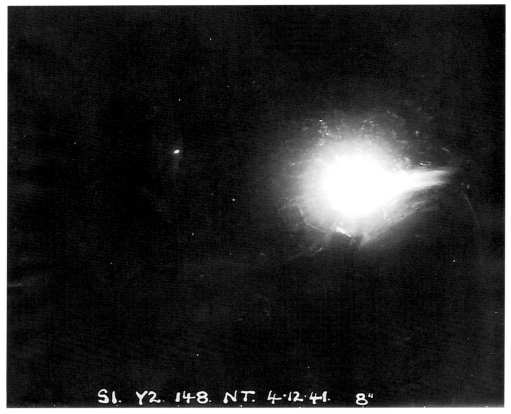

Bomb burst over Derna in a raid to disrupt and destroy the enemy supply route.

The mighty 4,000lb 'blockbusters' had to be treated with the utmost respect both on the ground and in the air.

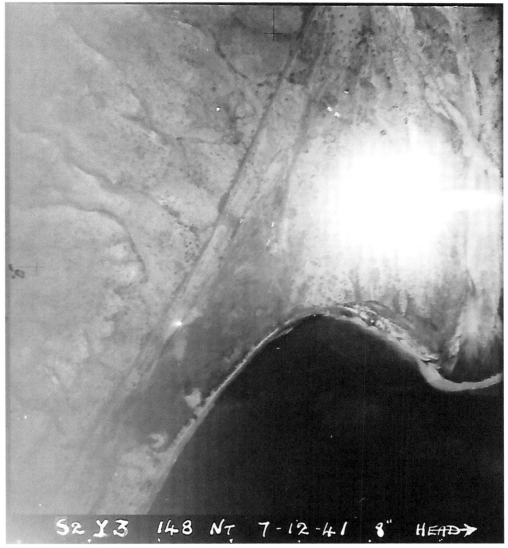

S2 Y3 148 NT 7-12-41 8" HEAD→

A 4,000lb bomb bursting at Ras Bu Meddad, eight kilometres west of Derna, on the night of 7 December 1941. Photographed from the Wellington of 'Jock' Baird.

الحكومة البريطانية‎

BRITISH GOVERNMENT

الى كل عربى كريم‎

السلام عليكم ورحمة الله وبركاته وبعد ، فحامل هذا الكتاب ضابط بالجيش البريطاني وهو صديق‎
وفى لكافة الشعوب العربية فنرجو أن تعاملوه بالطف والاكرام . وأن تحافظوا على حياته من كل‎
طارىء ، ونأمل عند الاضطرار أن تقدموا له مايحتاج اليه من طعام وشراب . وأن ترشدوه الى‎
أقرب معسكر بريطاني . وسنكافئكم مالياً بسخاء على ماتسدونه اليه من خدمات .‎
والسلام عليكم ورحمة الله وبركاته؟   القيادة البريطانية العامة في الشرق الاوسط‎

To All Arab Peoples — Greetings and Peace be upon you. The bearer of this letter is an
Officer of the British Government and a friend of all Arabs. Treat him well, guard him from
harm, give him food and drink, help him to return to the nearest British soldiers and you will
be rewarded. Peace and the Mercy of God upon you. The British High Command in the East.

SOME POINTS ON CONDUCT WHEN MEETING THE ARABS IN THE DESERT.

Remove footwear on entering their tents. Completely ignore their women. If thirsty drink
the water they offer, but DO NOT fill your waterbottle from their personal supply. Go to their
well and fetch what you want. Never neglect any puddle or other water supply for topping up
your bottle. Use the Halazone included in your Aid Box. Do not expect breakfast if you
sleep the night. Arabs will give you a mid-day or evening meal.

REMEMBER, NEVER TRY AND HURRY IN THE DESERT, SLOW AND SURE DOES IT.

A few useful words

English	Arabic	English	Arabic
English	Ingleezi	Day	Nahaar or Yom
Friend	Sa-hib, Sa-deek.	Night	Layl
Water	Moya	Half	Nuss
Food	Akl	Half a day	Nuss il Nahaar
Village	Balaad	Near	Gareeb
Tired	Ta-eban	Far	Baeed

Take me to the English and you will be rewarded.	Hud nee eind el Ingleez wa tahud Mu-ka-fa.
English Flying Officer	Za-bit Ingleezi Tye-yara
How far (how many kilos?)	Kam kilo ?
Enemy	Germani, Taliani, Siziliani

Distance and time: Remember, Slow & Sure does it

The older Arabs cannot read, write or tell the time. They measure distance by the number
of days journey. "Near" may mean 10 minutes or 10 hours. Far probably means over a days
journey. A days journey is probably about 30 miles. The younger Arabs are more accurate.

GOOD LUCK

John's 'Goolie Chit', a simple document to secure the help of local Arabs should he be brought down
in the desert or behind enemy lines.

The fluidity of the Desert War is amply illustrated in this shot of a former Luftwaffe airfield that is under new management.

Squadron Leader the Honourable Robert Baird. A charismatic and dynamic flight commander, 'Jock' Baird had a brief but spectacular war.

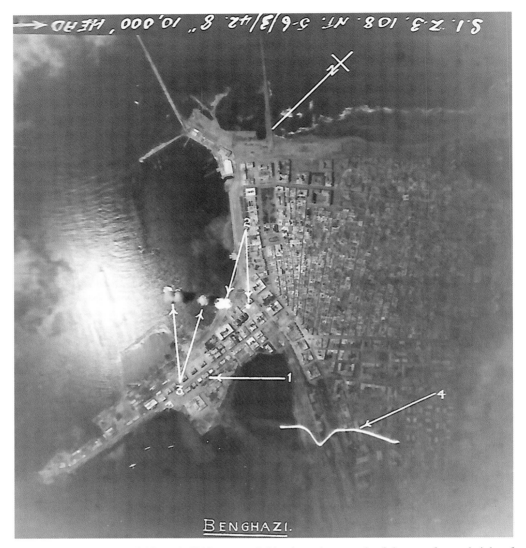

BENGHAZI.

Benghazi on the night of 5 March 1942, a remarkably clear photograph of the port from a height of 10,000ft and a series of bombs exploding in salvo.

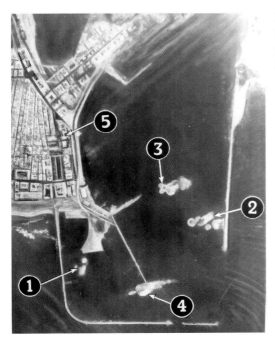

Benghazi, 9 April 1942. 1 is said to be a direct hit on a merchant ship; 5 is a direct hit on the former residence of the Italian Governor of Libya.

One of the first of the RAF Liberators to arrive in the Middle East. Their operational ceiling caused problems for the lower flying Wellingtons.

Another view of Benghazi and a large explosion (left) from 12,000ft.

A group of largely unheralded groundcrew 'out in the blue'. Much of their work had to be done by hand.

John and two of his contemporaries larking around for the camera. Dougie is standing guard while two German and Italian 'prisoners' pretend to flatten a new landing ground. John is playing the 'Italian', while a member of the groundcrew is the 'German'.

John and Angela in Scotland, 1943, while John was still a flight sergeant at 19 OTU as a screened wireless op.

The distinctive 'nose down' attitude of the Armstrong Whitworth Whitley, a workhorse of the operational training units.

Recently commissioned Pilot Officer Brennan, outside his father-in-law's home in Acton.

'Smithy'. Squadron Leader Duncan Hyland Smith (right), John's skipper for his second tour, a flight commander with 78 Squadron and later officer commanding 102 Squadron.

An unusual photograph taken on the ground of a 4,000lb blockbuster exploding.

An unnamed fitter sits precariously on the engine spinner of a Halifax at an airfield, 'somewhere in England'.

Devastation at the Rhine. This photo of an unnamed town shows the full extent of RAF and USAAF bombing.

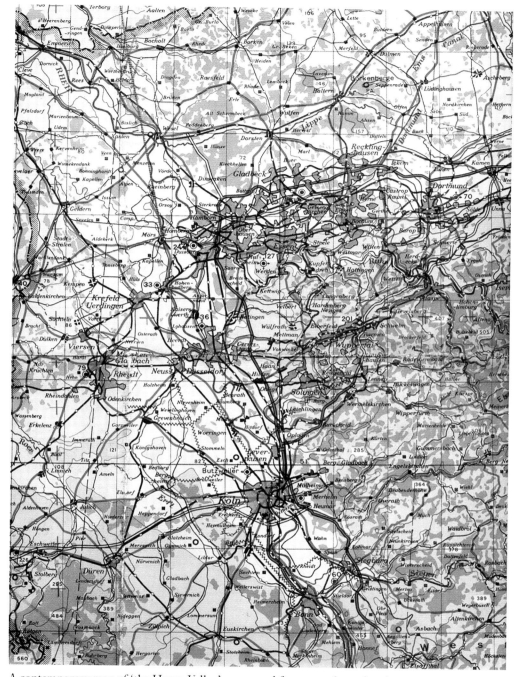

A contemporary map of 'the Happy Valley', graveyard for many a brave bomber crew.

John 1944. While never being afraid of war, the strain of operations appears etched on his face.

Flight Lieutenant John Brennan DFC at the war's end. Note his wireless operators flying brevet, first introduced in 1943.

A portrait of John in later life.

A gathering of no fewer than six DFCs. John is second from the right. Standing left is the late Tony Iveson, former Chairman of the Bomber Command Association. The photograph takes pride of place in John's dining room.

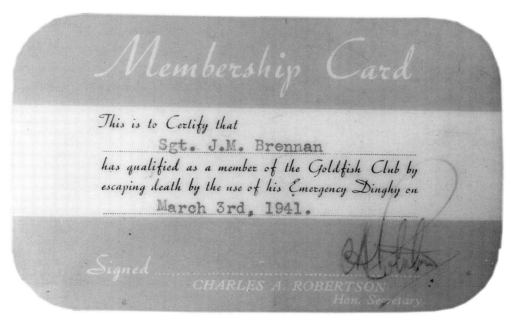

Membership Card

This is to Certify that

Sgt. J.M. Brennan

has qualified as a member of the Goldfish Club by escaping death by the use of his Emergency Dinghy on

March 3rd, 1941.

Signed

CHARLES A. ROBERTSON
Hon. Secretary

John's Goldfish Club Membership Badge. The date is a year out.

John's Distinguished Flying Cross and campaign medals, including the Africa Star and France and Germany Star.

John Brennan, May 2016, proudly holding his medals.

efforts and giving more time for the 'brown jobs' to retreat in good order.

The Squadron flew its last operation from ALG106 on the night of 25 June, the now familiar target of enemy troop and motorised transport concentrations in their sights. Seventeen aircraft took part. Flight Lieutenant William Hankin of 'A' Flight was obliged to crash land three quarters of a mile south east of Fuka railway station. A burst oil pipe was thought to be the cause. He had only been on the squadron for two days. Twenty-four hours later, orders were received for the squadron to withdraw. (Hankin received the DFC as squadron leader in February the following year.)

John packed up what few possessions he still had, including a handful of precious letters from home, and prepared to leave. Each squadron pilot was responsible not only for his own crew, but also the ground crew who crammed themselves and what little belongings they had into the confined space and bomb bays of each of the Wellingtons. Support staff and some of the heavier items would follow by road soon after. The evacuation almost went like clockwork. By midday, all but two of the aircraft had left for Kabrit: Squadron Leader Prickett took off at 14.00hrs; Pilot Officer Albert Loos – the last to leave – did not get away until three hours later, by which time Rommel's troops were almost knocking on the door for tea:

> We knew the Germans were very close but our aircraft had developed engine trouble some time previously and couldn't be fixed so the engine had to be replaced. Changing an engine in the desert, out in the open, is a complicated and time-consuming affair but our ground crews sweated through the morning and early afternoon to get it done.
>
> It would be usual (and safest) to fly an air test but there simply wasn't time. As soon as the final bolt had been tightened

on the engine cowling, we threw our kit on board, and I scrambled through to the front turret. The pilot started the engines, turned into wind and took off, hoping all the time that the engine fitters had done their jobs properly. He needn't have worried of course, although there was a moment as we thundered down the desert track, with the grit, sand and dust flying up behind us, that I thought we might never make it into the air. It was probably the only time I can really recall being scared. As it was we did make it safely into the air but only climbed to 2,000ft. The pilot seemed understandably reluctant to push the untried engine too far.

A few hours later and the Squadron was again on night operations from its new base.

*   *   *

For the first time in June, the 148 Squadron diarist began recording in detail the total numbers of operations flown and bombs dropped. It was impressive. For the period 25 June – 30 June, Squadron crews flew seventy-seven sorties comprising more than 424 operational hours and dropped 231,190lbs of bombs, nearly all in direct support of the Allied ground forces. Released from the dangerous monotony of the Benghazi 'mail run', and chiming with the reports in the official history[7], the crews revelled in the chance to do tangible damage to the German advance, and support their colleagues on the ground. They won deserved praise from their superiors, Tedder himself visiting the squadron on more than one occasion to impress upon the men the importance of their efforts. They also won a grudging respect from their enemy, continuous bombing causing considerable losses in men, tanks and fuel – the latter being crucial to sustaining the assault.

Operations were no less risky, however. On the last sortie of the month, Sergeant Hubert Kemball of 'A' Flight was flying Wellington DV568 with his crew when they were intercepted by a nightfighter. Enemy fire scythed through the rear turret, wounding the air gunner (Sergeant Williams) in the left arm and the left eye. Despite the damage, Kemball managed to make it back to base without further incident and see that his gunner received immediate hospitalisation. But for Kemball it was only a brief respite; he was killed two weeks later flying with a different gunner on an attack on Tobruk.[8]

With a new month came a new tactic, and an early form of Middle East pathfinding. The RAF began operating with their Fleet Air Arm (FAA) colleagues who would fly ahead of the bombers and mark the target using flares. The flares were dropped by crews from 821 and 826 Squadrons operating the Fairey Albercore, designed as a successor to the infinitely more famous Fairey Swordfish of 'Stringbag' fame. The Albercore was also a biplane and pleasant to fly. Although only available in small numbers, they did sterling service in further improving the accuracy and efficiency of bomber operations.

Continuous raids by day and by night played havoc with the German and Italian forces. The combined efforts of the Allied forces finally led the Desert Fox to order his army over to the defensive.

Tragedy befell the crew of Sergeant Clifford Handley, detailed for operations on the 7 July. As the 25-year-old Yorkshireman lifted the Wellington clear of the runway at Kabrit in the small hours of the morning, something went wrong, and the aircraft almost immediately crashed on the edge of Bitter Lake and exploded as it hit the water. By some miracle the rear turret was blown clear, with the air gunner (Sergeant J. E. Robinson) trapped inside. By some other miracle, the turret landed such that the gunner was upright and, although submerged, it was shallow enough for his head to remain above water. Help was soon at hand and Robinson was cut free and admitted to

Station Sick Quarters, suffering from minor cuts and abrasions, exposure, and the inevitable shock. The rest of the crew were killed.

The Squadron's run of bad luck continued the following evening with the loss of Flying Officer Frank Tribe, a 28-year-old married man from Hampshire, who failed to return from an attack on shipping in Tobruk Harbour. The aircraft was not located until two weeks later by members of the Egyptian Frontier Force who buried Tribe and the rest of the crew near to where the aircraft fell to earth.

Warrant Officer William Ross, one of the Squadron's Canadian pilots, almost went the same way as Sergeant Handley and his crew when he was obliged to force land in shallow water near to base. On 8 July his was one of twelve aircraft briefed once again to attack Tobruk. Two hours into their flight, the aircraft suffered instrument trouble and turned for home.

Unfortunately, Ross arrived back at base to find the airfield covered in ground mist, making a landing doubly difficult. Then, to add to his woes further, both of his engines cut through lack of fuel. The pilot lost sight of the aerodrome but still managed to bring the aircraft down safely over water. All of the crew escaped unhurt, though the Wellington was a Category II.[9]

Worse luck was to follow, for on the night of 11 July the Squadron lost two pilots and crews out of seven who were operating. Pilot Officer Peter Hoad and Flight Sergeant Kemball both failed to return. Kemball was killed, nothing of either pilot, aircraft or crew ever being found. There was better news for Hoad and his crew, however. Hit by flak over the target area, the pilot sent out a series of SOS messages as he fought to keep the aircraft in the air with an engine ablaze. With some luck and a large degree of skill, Hoad managed to bring the stricken aircraft down onto the beach where some of the crew attempted to make good their escape. Hoad chose to stay with his wounded rear gunner. All of the crew were captured soon after, to spend the remainder of the war in the bag.

For the next two weeks the Squadron continued to attack the ships off-loading vital supplies to the German forces. Poor visibility, heavy German flak and the occasional mechanical fault and pilot error notwithstanding, the results were remarkable, a significant tonnage of bombs being dropped and finding their target – at least if the reports from the post-op interrogations were to be believed. Pilot Officer Pearse crash-landed on his return from Tobruk on 14 July when he confused his flaps with the undercarriage controls and belly flopped without wheels. Flight Lieutenant James Brown, a 21-year-old married man from Leith in Scotland, went missing on the night of 16 July, nothing being heard or seen of the pilot, his crew or their aircraft from the moment they took off.

> *The wing commander once more urged us to 'press on' after a number of crews returned with their bombs still on board, unable to locate the target in the gloom or otherwise suffering technical difficulties. Discipline was under pressure again but held, at least for the time being. It looked like there would not be a mutiny this time.*

On 24 July, a Wellington of 108 Squadron was being bombed up when a 40lb incendiary exploded, killing or seriously injuring five of the groundcrew. Flying debris set fire to at least two other aircraft that were subsequently destroyed. Three days later, on 27 July, John's tour at last came to an end. In the event, however, his posting proved to be only temporary:

> *I'd received orders to proceed to the Personnel Despatch Centre (PDC) and told I would be going home, that I had done enough. It was a strange feeling to think that it was all over, and yet the fighting was still going on. I was not there for long before my*

posting was cancelled with immediate effect, and I was told to report back to Kabrit. Rommel, it appeared, was still a threat and they needed all the experienced men they could get!

It would be another two weeks before the plug was finally pulled on John's first tour, a period of intense air operations where two sorties a night were not uncommon for the already exhausted crews. Groundcrews worked tirelessly through the night to re-fuel, re-arm and re-bomb their charges, often in total darkness, usually in the open and exposed to the elements.

Aircraft were now regularly returning with battle damage, as the Germans increased the defences around the port of Tobruk to protect their merchant ships. There was also considerable movement on the ground as the Germans attempted to ship vital supplies to the front line along the dusty roads from the port:

All of these bomber operations tended to be at low level, often less that 2,000ft or so, with orders to bomb and machine gun anything we saw on the ground that moved. I let go several times. It was relatively easy to pick out the transport against the desert and you almost couldn't miss. We would fire mixed ammunition so that every half a dozen or so rounds was a tracer so that we could see we were hitting the target. Of course it was relatively safe as they had little to fire back at us other than small arms fire.

In those final days of John's time in the Middle East, the Squadron suffered further sad injury and loss. On 29 July, Flight Sergeant Wild returned to base with a dead rear gunner (33-year-old Sergeant David Lewis), killed by nightfighter attack. They had been intercepted by what they believed to be a Junkers 88 while on their bombing run four miles east of Tobruk. The ground crews were left with the unpleasant task of washing the blood and remains from the turret the next day. Twenty-four hours later, Wellington ES991 flown by a New Zealand NCO crashed into the Little Bitter Lake, the pilot having been unable to maintain height. Although the pilot and most of the crew made it clear with only cuts and bruises, one of the gunners (20-year-old Londoner Sergeant John Chandler) was concussed and drowned, his friends powerless to save him. It was the pilot's first trip as captain; it was not a happy one.[10]

Pilot Officer William Bohl, a 20-year-old Queenslander and his crew failed to return from operations on the night of 31 July. Bohl and his four crew, including two Canadians, were all killed. At the beginning of August, Sergeant Herbert Tricks found himself in difficulty over the battle area when an engine cut. Losing height rapidly they followed the now usual pattern of ditching anything not bolted down in order to save weight. It worked for a short time before the aircraft finally gave in to the laws of gravity and crashed, injuring two of the crew in the process. Fortunately, they managed to attract help, the injured airmen being rescued by Lysander and the remainder returning by lorry. (Tricks later went on to be awarded the DFM and was commissioned. He was killed as a flying instructor at 11 OTU in January 1945.)

At the beginning of the second week of August, John was finally posted out, his work in the Middle East completed. He had flown more than forty operations comprising a remarkable 296 operational hours and survived, despite the best that the German and Italians could throw at him. He had been lucky; many had not.

Now at last it was time to return home, and an uncertain future.

Chapter 5

Homeward Bound

John was ordered to report to GHQ Cairo to be processed and given the necessary paperwork and instructions to return home. The headquarters had somewhat calmed since its earlier hiatus. There were no longer any confidential papers burning in the grate:

> *When I arrived I was given a passport application to fill out and then taken downstairs into a courtyard where a photographer was waiting to take my picture. They gave me a jacket to wear so that I looked more like a civilian. I was told to report back the next day, so I had a night to myself in Cairo.*
>
> *Twenty-four hours later I was handed a five-year passport, dated 11 August 1942, and allowing me to pass freely throughout the British Empire, Egypt, Sudan, Portugal, and all 'French, Belgian and Portuguese Possessions'. It gave my profession, somewhat amusingly, as 'government official.' I didn't think it would fool anyone.*

With the precious document in his pocket, John learned that he was being given passage in a BOAC (formerly Imperial Airways) flying boat, and flying a route that would take him across dangerous and inhospitable lands to safety. Happily, he was in one of the most reliable long-range aircraft of its time, a Shorts S30 Empire (coded G – AFKZ and named 'Cathay', it had been delivered to Imperial Airways in March 1940), capable of speeds of up to 170kts and a range of more than 700 nautical miles. There were around twenty passengers in the group, all wrapped up in their own thoughts; all aware of their own particular responsibilities:

> *We took off and headed south and landed at the famous city of Khartoum, in the Sudan, where the White Nile and Blue Nile converge. Finding water was of course very important in a flying boat! Some hours later the following morning we took off again and landed at Stanleyville (now Kisangani, the capital of the Orientale Province of the Democratic Republic of Congo) where we spent the night. The following day we took off for Leopoldville (now Kinshasa), still in what was then the Belgian Congo.*

Landing in the Belgian Congo was a strange, almost cinematic experience for a young Irishman from the country. Natives in dugout canoes paddled out to greet them, chanting as they did so in their base voices, plunging their paddles to a hypnotic rhythm that propelled them quickly through the water.

> *Our next leg took us to Lagos (in Nigeria) where we spent another night before flying on to Freetown. En route we picked up another passenger who was introduced to us as the Minister of the Interior of South Africa. From Freetown we then flew our penultimate leg and another long haul to Lisbon in Portugal where we were met by an official of the British Embassy. It was 19 August. Portugal was of course neutral and full of German spies, so I was given £5 spending money and told not to talk to anyone! I checked in to a small hotel, unpacked what few possessions I had and then set out to explore the sights and delights of the city.*

John spent a day in Lisbon before again taking off for the last leg to Ireland, the flying boat at last easing gently down upon the waters of the harbour at Foynes in the mouth of the Shannon Estuary and clearing customs at the newly-opened Shannon Airport. The date was 20 August.

After a brief stop over for breakfast, the boat continued for the comparatively short hop to Poole in Dorset, John finally putting his feet on English soil for the first time in almost a year. Having been issued with a railway warrant and a few days leave, he entrained to London to be reunited with his wife and her family.

* * *

If John thought that the RAF would have any sympathy for a man who had been absent for so long he was sorely mistaken. The Air Ministry's decisions could, on occasion, border on the perverse. While there were jobs aplenty for tour-expired aircrew, in any number of Operational Training Units in England, John was posted to RAF Kinloss in the north of Scotland. It is difficult to imagine a place in the United Kingdom further away from London and his bride. To make matters worse, John was posted as a screened wireless instructor, despite having had little or no experience of wireless since becoming operational.

RAF Kinloss, near the Moray Firth, was home to 19 OTU. The Unit had been formed in May 1940, originally as part of 6 (Training) Group, converting crews to fly the twin-engined Armstrong Whitworth Whitley – then one of the mainstays of Bomber Command and the principal aircraft flown by 4 Group in the north.

By 1942, and now part of 91 Group[1] (the group had been re-named in March 1942), training was being conducted both from Kinloss and later its satellite, RAF Forres. The once front-line Whitley had now been relegated (primarily) to a training role, the Mark V (the major production variant with Merlin X engines and a stretched fuselage) being the most prevalent alongside the ubiquitous 'Faithful Annie'.

On John's arrival he reported to the adjutant, as usual, and was directed to meet the signals leader, Flight Lieutenant 'Dusty' Miller. He learned he was to be one of five 'screened' wireless ops and quickly made friends with two them: 'Happy' Hanson and 'Jolly' Jenkins. (It is not known whether the nicknames were in any way ironic!). They appeared to be inseparable, and wherever they went, mischief was never far behind. Miller, on the other hand, was more difficult to read:

> *From what I learned, Miller had already completed an operational tour, like me, and so was clearly a very experienced Signals Leader. But he was another one who was always a little aloof and unpredictable. He never said much, if at all, and had a habit of looking right through you, as though he were constantly weighing you up and anticipating what you might say in return.*

That evening, John also caught his first glimpse of the Chief Instructor, Wing Commander Giles, and the Station Commander, Group Captain Jarman. Both were imposing figures, and both wearing decorations for gallantry beneath their rather faded pilot wings. Leonard Giles had picked up the DFC with 115 Squadron, not long before being 'rested'. (Giles would later add the AFC for his time as an instructor, and the OBE and a Queen's Commendation for Valuable Service in the Air before retiring from the service as a group captain.) As OC he was in charge of all of the day-to-day and operational aspects of flying.

Group Captain Geoffrey Jarman, meanwhile, wore not only the DFC but also the DSO, an award he had earned leading a section of Halifax aircraft to attack the battleship Scharnhorst on a famous attack at La Pallice in July 1941. A kiwi from Ashburton, Jarman's credentials for commanding 19 OTU were impeccable. Having joined the Service in 1929 and flown fighters with 19 Squadron, much of his early career had in fact been as a qualified flying instructor. He had also experienced operational command, being in charge of 77 Squadron in August 1940 and 76 Squadron in May 1941. He had taken over command of the station at Kinloss in October 1943 from Group Captain Potter, having previously been the Training Wing's commanding officer. His place was in turn taken by Wing Commander David MacNair.[2]

Jarman was a stickler for discipline and had two obsessions: the first was planning for gas attacks. If you did not react quickly enough, or worse, were too slow to get out of bed and were caught, then you could expect to be taken down to the decontamination hut and doused down with cold water.

His second obsession was making sure that the maximum number of aircraft were airborne at any one time. Even after heavy snowfalls, all of the non-commissioned officers and airmen were sent out with shovels to help clear the runways. It was back breaking. It seemed that no matter what the conditions were, we always had to fly, to the point that I'm not convinced it was responsible or safe.

As John suggests, it could be dangerous work. On more than one occasion, John remembers an aircraft icing up and crashing near the field. While this might be expected at height and in the colder air, at Kinloss it could happen when the aircraft was only a few hundred feet above the ground, with potentially fatal consequences.

Only a week or so after John arrived, an Anson flown by Sergeant Llewellyn flew into a mountain (Mount Macdui – the second highest mountain in the UK after Ben Nevis), killing everyone on board. A few days later, on 3 September, a Whitley crashed on take-off when an engine cut, again killing all of the crew. Other crews who found themselves in difficulty were more fortunate. One Canadian pilot on a night cross-country became so hopelessly lost when the wireless failed that he and his crew took to their parachutes and returned to face the commander's wrath.

Death, however, became the pattern of life at Kinloss and indeed at all training establishments where novice pilots and aircrew found themselves in unfamiliar aircraft and situations without sufficient experience to manage. In the month of September 1942 alone, some eighteen men from 19 OTU had been killed or injured in accidents. And some of the losses were especially tragic. On 16 October, another Canadian pilot was on a searchlight co-operation exercise when he went missing, never to be seen again, officially 'lost without trace'. It is strongly suspected that he fell victim to one of our own nightfighters who claimed to have shot down an enemy aircraft in the vicinity where the bomber was operating.

Even the more experienced pilots could be caught out, especially by extreme weather conditions. A violent electrical storm on the night of 29 October caused two of the unit's aircraft to crash, one flown by 21-year-old Flight Sergeant James Williams whose Whitley was struck by lightning. Williams was a screened pilot who had earlier flown with 115 Squadron and been awarded an immediate DFM for a particularly hazardous trip to Bremen a few months earlier in which he had brought his damaged aircraft home at 100ft and landed without flaps and with only one engine working. It was a cruel twist that a pilot of such vast and exceptional skill should lose his life in the comparative safety of a training establishment. It was perhaps even more ironic that the second pilot to crash that night, who was yet to fly his first operation, should survive. John remembers these incidents well:

On the station there was always a crew on twenty-four hour duty. This meant that if any aircraft should find itself in difficulty, there was an experienced crew on hand to give assistance, should it be needed. We operated a rota, and you were usually told at least two weeks in advance when you were required.

On one particular night, I was meant to be on duty but for some reason it went clean out of my head. At the end of the day's training, I returned home as usual to spend the evening with my wife who had come north to join me. At some point in the middle of the night, quite a storm blew up and two of our aircraft found themselves in trouble. The duty crew was dutifully summoned and arrived, minus one wireless op.

A message was broadcast on the Tannoy for Flight Sergeant Brennan to report to Flying Control and repeated every few minutes. Of course Flight Sergeant Brennan did not hear it as he was safely tucked up in bed off site. The following morning when I reported for duty, my flight commander was somewhat irate and said: 'where the hell have you been? Don't you realise you kept the whole station awake for half the night?' He said a few more things besides and left me by saying that the station commander was livid and that whatever happened to me was now out of his hands.

I was understandably nervous for the rest of the day, convinced that this was going to be a Court Martial offence. It probably deserved to be. I waited and waited but for some reason the call never came. I never missed duty again.

After the loneliness and extreme desert conditions of the Middle East that had sapped at John's energy, Kinloss brought its own drab weariness and monotony. But there was the occasional incident to cheer, one involving another screened pilot called 'Davy' Dunlop:

Davy was the spitting image of Jimmy Edwards, the comedian and raconteur, with his splendid whiskers and jovial face. He was an ex-bomber pilot, an accomplished flyer, and a bit of a devil. On cross-country exercises with pupil navigators flying in Ansons and Whitleys over Scotland, he'd ask me whether the trailing aerial was in. As soon as he did that, I knew that it was his cue for some crazy flying. He would push the stick forward, plunge down like a Stuka, then the engine would cut out and he would zoom up again with the engines re-engaged, scaring the hell out of the shepherds and the sheep below as well as his pupils in the aircraft.

On one occasion there was a party of Ghurkhas training in nearby Aviemore, and we received a request from one of the authorities as to whether we would take them up in one of our aircraft. The great day arrived and a dozen or so of these small but fierce warriors turned up with their officer and clambered onboard a Whitley. There were no seats as such, so we placed them on each side of the fuselage and they crouched down, half a dozen on each side.

Davy looked at me, winked and said, 'I'll give them a fight to remember', and did just that. As soon as we were out into the countryside and well away from any hills or mountains, Davy started putting the aircraft through its paces, making the Whitley perform stunts that I didn't think it was capable of. He particularly liked to pull the nose up and down in a bucking motion, throwing the poor old Ghurkhas about the place like sailors on a ship in a storm. Not surprisingly, by the time we landed every one of them had been sick, and our ground crew were not best pleased at having to clear up the mess.[3]

Accidents were frequent and could sometimes be spectacular. A Whitley V was written off, for example, when an Anson landed on top of it! The Anson, somewhat bent but otherwise complete, was gently lifted from its precarious position and repaired, but not before a now-famous photograph of the incident had been captured for prosperity.

Occasionally the air raid siren would send the airmen scuttling to the gun pits and shelters, alerted to a potential intruder – a Junkers 88 more often than not wandering too close to the airfield – but in reality the fledgling crews were more at risk from the unpredictable weather, the driving rain, sleet and snow and the occasional gale than enemy aircraft. Kinloss did have its fair share of visitors, however: Lancasters, Halifaxes, Fortresses, Liberators, Hudsons, Mosquitos, Spitfires and Defiants are all types recorded in the ORB as passing through, or landing in a state of emergency. Where needed, the senior medical officer, Squadron Leader Robert Munro MB Ch.B and his team were on hand to give assistance. Among the more prestigious names to be entered into the visitors' book was Wing Commander Basil Robinson, who had been an early exponent of the Halifax as OC 35 Squadron, and who had similarly been involved in attacking the Scharnhorst. The two had a great deal in common, not least their bravery.

Aside from the distracting gas attack and superfluous invasion exercises, and the occasional excitement of the station's ground defences opening up on one of their own aircraft, it did not take long for John to settle into a routine. Kinloss was one of the busier OTUs and there was a constant flow of aircrew reaching the penultimate stage of their training.

My duties were to fly with trainee wireless ops who had part qualified from the wireless school and prepare them for operational flying. This meant teaching them how to keep a log and to confirm that all entries to the log were properly and accurately timed. It included showing them how to make contact with various HF/DF stations to obtain a bearing or fix, what to do in an emergency, and the procedures for descending through cloud. At Kinloss, the latter exercise was particularly important as cloud was a constant danger.

John and Angela rented a room in Forres, which was a satellite to Kinloss, and spent many happy times together with another couple with whom they shared a kitchen. They later rented a room above the post office in the High Street, again they shared certain facilities, though this time with one of the staff pilots on the base who came to a rather unfortunate end:

He took off one day in an Anson and sometime later his aircraft was seen to crash into the hills killing everyone on board. I believe he was responsible for the sergeants' mess funds and the rumour was that some of those funds had gone missing. Whether that is true or not is difficult to say, but I do remember that his wife was in a terrible state at the time. It was one of the more difficult issues of having wives close by. The day after the accident, I was the wireless operator who flew with the Investigating Officer to the crash scene to see if there were any clues as to what had happened. Of course there was not a great deal to see apart from the shattered remains of what had once been an aircraft and its crew. It was a pitiful sight.

John's happiness with his new posting was given a further boost with the arrival of his good friend, Joe Brookes:

I couldn't quite believe it when Joe turned up on the station. He had been with me out in the Middle East, though with 108 Squadron at Kabrit, and injured badly when forced to bail out from his stricken bomber. He told me that his parachute had been seen coming down by a rear-guard of Australian soldiers who set out, at great risk to themselves, to rescue him. He was subsequently airlifted to Tel Aviv for treatment. He was now fully recovered and arrived with his wife. We enjoyed many long walks and the occasional jar.[4]

At the beginning of 1943, John was formally promoted temporary flight sergeant, a 'crown' being sewn above his sergeant's stripes. A few months later he was summoned to see the Signals Leader, 'Dusty' Miller, and told he was going to be put forward for a commission. Indeed, the recommendation had already been made, and he was told to expect an interview with the station commander. Straight away the memory of the 'stormy night' came into his mind, and he doubted whether his application would even get past first base. He was also concerned because he knew that after his somewhat chaotic departure from the Middle East, his Service Record was not all it could have been, and there were certain 'gaps' in his movements. In the event he need not have worried:

When the day of my interview arrived my mind was quite quickly put at rest when, rather than reminding me what had happened, he simply asked me a series of questions about my tour of operations in the Middle East and my view of the current war situation. He also asked about my knowledge of Air Force Law and the King's Regulations and with that, the interview ended. A day or so later I was informed that I would now be interviewed by the Air Officer Commanding (AOC)[5] *who took it upon himself to speak to anyone hoping to become an officer. It was then not until November that I was eventually told to report to Group HQ, and informed that I was to relinquish my flight sergeant's crown and stripes and my NCO status on appointment to a commission.*

Thus, on 17 November 1943, John officially became Pilot Officer Brennan, whereupon he received a voucher for £50 towards the cost of his uniform and other essential officer's items, and a train ticket to London to ensure he became properly attired:

> *When I arrived back at Kinloss from London, I was walking towards the flight office and an airman was strolling towards me. As he drew level he snapped the smartest salute which I returned. I knew then that I was an officer!*

John's pleasure at his promotion was followed by news that he and his wife were expecting their first child or, as it turned out, their first children, as Angela was pregnant with twins. Sadly, their happiness was short lived. In the first week of April 1944, Angela developed septicaemia; on the fifteenth of the month, twin girls were born, but sadly one died shortly after:

> *The matron of the hospital 'phoned and said that she wanted to see me. She explained, in detail, what had happened and advised me to have our second surviving baby baptised. I was scheduled to fly on two Anson training flights that night and so went to see the Signals Leader to explain my position. I told him about my wife's medical condition and asked if I could be excused duty that night. He refused, telling me that I should not allow my private life to interfere with the good running of the station or with my responsibilities as an instructor. It seemed particularly cruel and unnecessary, but I was in no position to argue with him.*

The first flight went off without a hitch; taking off shortly after 20.00hrs, a two-hour trip across the Moray Firth to the Western Isles and back. It was on the second flight that disaster struck:

On our return a north-easterly storm blew up and the pilot, Warrant Officer Paddy Clark, decided when we reached Fraserburgh that we would fly along the coast and then back to base. It was a route that should take us past Banff and Lossiemouth if all went well.

I was in the main body of the aircraft, supervising the trainee wireless operator and happened to look out of the window. I could see lights, and decided I had better tell the pilot that for whatever reason we had to be considerably more inland than he had thought. Given that we were only at a height of about 2,000ft, we were in danger of hitting a mountain.

No sooner had I the thought than it happened. We hit the deck with an almighty crack, the aircraft almost bouncing on its belly as we skimmed across the top of a hill. The force was such that the navigator was thrown forward into the nose and I finished up on top of him in a heap.

It took me a few moments to come to my senses and take stock. Nobody seemed to be too badly hurt and the wireless set was still working so when I had recovered my senses I sent out an emergency message to the control station at Inverness and informed them that we had crashed but from what I could tell there were no serious injuries. They told me that help was on its way and to sit tight. I grabbed the fire axe and cut the door open so that we would not be trapped inside in case of fire, and then we waited.

As dawn broke I could make out an ambulance below, and a mountain rescue team on their way up to help us. With their help we managed to make our own way down. It was only by chance that none of us was killed. After a short check up in the medical centre, I was allowed home. Shortly afterwards Angela was also discharged from the hospital.

* * *

John spent almost two years at Kinloss before his time in Training Command came to an end. The first course he had tutored on his arrival was No 45 comprising seventy men: fourteen pilots; fourteen observers; fourteen air bombers; fourteen wireless operators; and fourteen air gunners. His final Course was No 85. In that time he flew almost 600 hours to bring his total to 1061.45. He survived three station commanders, and a similar number of OCs.

Jarman was posted out in April 1943 to RAF Wyton, his place being taken by Group Captain Francis Swain OBE, AFC. Swain was typically 'old school' but there was not much he did not know about flying, having joined the RAF in 1922. Not only was he an experienced instructor, but also a test pilot of some renown, setting a new world altitude record in 1936 while flying a Bristol 138A.

Swain was posted to 8 Group PFF and superseded by Group Captain Robert Cole in October. Cole, like Jarman, had the benefit of operational experience and command. He had attracted some controversy early in the war as Officer Commanding 9 Squadron for the raid in December 1939, when five of his pilots were shot down on a disastrous daylight reconnaissance to Wilhelmshaven. Subsequently mentioned in despatches on at least three separate occasions however, there can be little doubting his bravery.

It was Group Captain Cole who signed John's confidential report at the end of his time in Kinloss (dated 26 May 1944) confirming the remarks made by the 19 OTU commanding officer, Wing Commander John Forbes, describing John rather disparagingly as 'an officer of average ability' who was 'quite sound technically but lacks personality and possesses little tendency to leadership'. (Forbes had been posted in on 19 October 1943 at the same time as the new station commander. It was in effect a changing of the guard, Forbes taking over from Wing Commander Thomas Bingham-Hall who left to take command of 156 Squadron Pathfinder Force. Forbes was later awarded the Air Force

Cross for his time in Training Command and added a DFC having returned to operations with 77 Squadron as that unit's last wartime commanding officer.)

John received orders to report to a Heavy Conversion Unit (HCU) at Riccall in North Yorkshire in preparation for a return to operations with a front line squadron.

In two years the war had taken a significant turn in favour of the Allies. The Germans had been defeated in North Africa, the Italians had surrendered, and the Russians were sweeping the Axis forces from the motherland. Most who knew about such things understood that victory was now almost certain. A Second Front was imminent; it was simply a matter of time, and achieving success with the least number of casualties.

The RAF had also changed beyond recognition. In 1940 there were only 11 Operational Training Units; by 1942, that number had doubled and by the beginning of 1944, the OTUs were turning out many hundreds of trained aircrew every week, primarily to fill the ranks of Bomber Command.

Indeed, Bomber Command was the least recognisable. The 'make do and mend' mentality that had seen crews sent out in ill-suited aircraft to bomb targets in northern Europe with fewer than ten hours' night-flying experience had been replaced by a force of highly-trained, well-equipped squadrons capable of overwhelming German defences on a scale that would rival today's tactics of 'shock and awe'.

When John had left the UK for the Middle East in the autumn of 1941, Bomber Command could muster only forty-four squadrons of which thirty-eight were operational. It had short of 400 serviceable aircraft and crews. On paper it had more, but in reality it could seldom raise a force of more than 300 aircraft for one night's operations. By the beginning of 1944, Bomber Command had expanded to become a weapon of terrifying force, capable of putting more than 1,000 aircraft in the air on a regular basis and laying waste to great swathes of enemy occupied land.

Bomber Command had a new leader, new equipment, and new aircraft. At the helm was its Commander-in-Chief, Arthur Harris, who was vigorously pursuing his superiors' plans to destroy German morale and the will and capability to fight through area bombing. In terms of new equipment it had 'Gee', a new technology that could help navigators more accurately find their target. For new aircraft, now all of its heavy bomber squadrons were equipped with four-engined aircraft – most notably the Avro Lancasters and Handley Page Halifaxes – capable of dropping a huge tonnage of bombs on German cities, reaping the whirlwind that Harris had promised.

The command structure had needed to expand to manage the increased volume of aircraft and men now at Harris' disposal. It comprised: 1 Group, under the command of Air Vice Marshal Edward Rice with his headquarters at Bawtry Hall; 3 Group under Air Vice Marshal Richard Harrison at Exning; 5 Group under Air Vice Marshal Sir Ralph Cochrane, a favourite of Harris, headquartered at Morton Hall near Swinderby; 6 Group, unique in that it was an all-Canadian Group, under Air Vice Marshal 'Black Mike' McEwen at Allerton Park; and 8 Group Pathfinder Force, based at Castle Hill House and led by the controversial Australian, Air Vice Marshal Donald Bennett.

In the north, with airfields all over Yorkshire, was 4 Group, under the command of Air Vice Marshal Roddy Carr, a Kiwi. Originally headquartered at Linton-on-Ouse before the war, the Group staff had moved to Heslington Hall in the Spring of 1940.

The training organisation had similarly needed to keep pace with changing demands. To start, Conversion Flights had been formed within each squadron to convert crews to new types. Now the OTUs had been supplemented with dedicated Heavy Conversion Units (HCUs) to convert novice pilots from two engines onto four. So-called 'Finishing Schools' for those who would be operating the Avro Lancaster had also been created.

The airfield at Riccall had been built in 1942 and opened at the end of the year as a satellite to RAF Marston Moor. Although officially open for business in December 1942, the Halifax conversion units of 76 and 78 squadrons had moved in three months prior in September. The following month they formally merged to form 1658 Heavy Conversion Unit and soon after they were joined by 10 Conversion Flight from Melbourne, 102 Conversion Flight from Pocklington, and 158 Conversion Flight from Rufforth, bringing the establishment up to thirty-two Halifax aircraft. The Officer Commanding was Henry (Harry) Drummond AFC, DFM. Drummond, a former NCO, was an early exponent of the Halifax, winning the DFM in 1941 with 76 Squadron.

A terrible tragedy had befallen the men and women at Riccall just a few days before John's arrival. On the night of 10 May, a Halifax II was being flown by a young Australian and his crew on a night exercise when it crashed into the spire of St James' Church in Selby. The debris and fireball that resulted smashed down onto the houses below with terrible consequences. As well as the 21-year-old captain (Flight Sergeant Thomas Laver RAAF) and six-man crew, fourteen civilians were either killed or seriously injured, including a baby. (The memories of that day and the effects of the crash are still felt in the local community seventy years later.)

John arrived as a newly promoted flying officer[6] at Riccall on 2 June and quickly worked out the lie of the land. Riccall was like any number of RAF stations built for the war, with its three concrete and asphalt runways, and its familiar T2 and B1 hangers that offered some protection from the elements for the groundcrews to service and maintain the aircraft.

As a second-tour man, John was unusual but by no means unique; what perhaps set him apart more was that he was an officer, and commissioned wireless ops were few and far between. He was also a spare bod, and not yet part of a crew. Typically, aircrew passing through conversion training had already formed their own homogenous units, and most often as a crew of five. At HCU they would become seven, picking up a second air gunner (both the Lancaster and the Halifax had mid-upper as well as rear turrets) and a flight engineer, a comparatively new 'trade' that had been established with the introduction of the four-engined 'heavies'. In John's case, he and a number of other 'odds and sods' were gathered in a room and the pilots came to take their pick. With his new skipper, John struck gold:

> *His name was Hyland-Smith and he insisted I call him 'Smithy'. In return he called me 'Paddy' for obvious reasons, and it stuck. He had lived, I believe, in Northern Rhodesia and had served as an instructor, so he had a huge number of flying hours in his log. He was also already a squadron leader so I knew that wherever we were posted, he would most likely be one of the flight commanders and we would be one of the senior crews.*

Originally from Oxford, Duncan Frank Hyland-Smith had learned to fly before the war, and in February 1938 was selected among the first contingent of Rhodesians to be chosen for a short service commission with the RAF. The 20-year-old was immediately marked out as a gifted pilot and with the right temperament to become an instructor. Having completed an instructor's course at the Central Flying School, he went on to fly with 614 (County of Glamorgan) Squadron which at the time was equipped with the Lysander, an army co-operation aircraft that later found fame with the Special Operations Executive (SOE), dropping and picking up agents in France. While with 614 he was obliged to make an emergency landing while flying a Hawker Hind and escaped serious injury, despite the aircraft turning over on its nose. Posted to Vereerniging in South Africa, he spent almost two years instructing at a series of Service Flying Training Schools (SFTS) and Air Schools before returning to the UK and being placed on the Reserve. He did not have to wait long until his services were once again called upon, but this time in an operational capacity.

'Smithy' introduced John to the rest of the crew: the navigator, 'Shep' Shepherd, a quiet Canadian; the air bomber, Isherwood, an achiever who liked to work and play hard; the rear gunner, Peter Bradbury, always one for a line-shoot; and the mid-upper gunner, Nelson, who always had an eye for the women. Completing the crew was the flight engineer, S.G. Littler. All, with the exception of the flight engineer, were commissioned.

The crew took their turn on the training roster, undertaking all manner of practice flights to hone their individual skills and 'gel' as part of a crew. Cross countries, night-time navigation, air-to-sea firing, and fighter affiliation exercises were complemented by specific flying training for the principal benefit of the pilot. These included circuits and bumps and practice landings. Perhaps because of his vast flying experience, 'Smithy' took to the Halifax like the proverbial duck to water. Others struggled, accidents happened.[7]

Some accidents were perhaps more understandable than others for a fledgling pilot attempting to master the intricacies of four-engined flight. Three-engined landings, for example, caused more than their fair share of troubles. Getting the approach speed right such that the heavy bomber didn't stall was a particular challenge, even with an experienced instructor alongside. Closing the throttles too early could spell disaster.

Other accidents were unexplained, and some crews simply vanished without trace. The aircraft of Pilot Officer Ronald Giles RAAF, a

28-year-old from South Australia, is a case in point. He set out in Halifax JD462 for an innocuous air-sea firing exercise and was never seen or heard from again.

Occasionally, and too often in the minds of some, the aircraft let them down, both on the ground and in the air. A Canadian pilot, Sergeant Patrick McBrinn, had returned from a morning fighter affiliation exercise and was taxiing back to dispersal when his brakes failed. He was powerless to prevent the heavy bomber from crashing into a tree. ('Mac' McBrinn was later killed on operations with 76 Squadron.)

Flight Lieutenant A.D. Andrew was instructing his pupil pilot on the niceties of three-engined flying when he had the horror of seeing the starboard inner propeller spin away, but not before it had damaged two of the remaining three engines. Thus, with only one engine working fully, and in a magnificent feat of airmanship, he managed to bring the Halifax down for a forced landing, earning the praise of his commanding officer and the eternal gratitude of his pupil. He also received a green endorsement in his log book.

In a Halifax, John was once more at the front of the aircraft with a grandstand view, although not in the front turret. Unlike the Lancaster, where the wireless operator sat behind the pilot, in a Halifax the pilot's seat was on a raised platform, with the wireless op seated immediately below. It was said to make for better communication. It also meant that it was quicker to make the front escape hatch should they be shot down. Comparisons between the Halifax and the Lancaster are invidious; the Halifax had one critical advantage, however: it was easier to escape from in an emergency.

'Smithy' and his crew came through their training unscathed, despite the dangers, and despite the quirks of the Halifax IIs that could be difficult to control:

The Halifax had a habit of swinging alarmingly on take-off, which the skipper had to correct with forceful use of the rudder bars to keep us straight and level on the runway. I would fly on every occasion that Smithy took to the air, even for practice circuits and bumps, so I could make contact with base in case of emergency.

At the end of their six-week conversion, the flight commander signed their log books, endorsed by the Officer Commanding, to show that they had passed the course with flying colours. As a crew they were posted briefly to 102 Squadron at Pocklington. Within a matter of days, however, they were heading twenty miles south to Breighton and their new home, 78 Squadron. It gloried under the motto: *Nemo Non Paratus* – Nobody Unprepared.

Chapter 6

Nobody Unprepared

Originally allocated to Home Defence when it was formed at Newhaven in November 1916, 78 Squadron spent the first part of the Great War forlornly chasing elusive Zeppelins up and down the south coast in out–of–date BE2 bi–planes before moving to London to protect the capital. It had just started to re-equip with the more modern (for the time) Sopwith one-and-a-half Strutters when the war to end all wars finally came to an end.

As with so many other similar units, the squadron was quickly disbanded and did not reform until 1936, when 'B' Flight of 10 Squadron at Boscombe Down was retitled and given new squadron status. On this occasion it was earmarked for a bombing role, becoming part of the newly created 4 Group and flying Handley Page Heyford bombers, an enormous bi-plane throwback to an earlier generation. In the summer of 1937 it began re-equipping with the infinitely more modern Whitley, and at the start of the war it was tasked with training newly formed crews prior to posting to their front line squadrons. It flew its first raid in anger in July 1940, just as the Spitfire and Hurricane pilots of Fighter Command were earning the plaudits at the start of the Battle of Britain.

It had its fair share of bomber alumni within its ranks during that time, including Wing Commander Basil Robinson, the regular visitor to Kinloss and later a noted Pathfinder, who made a spectacular solo flight home after a raid on Turin with OC 35 Squadron. His flares had hung up over the Alps and ignited with potentially devastating consequences. Fearing the worst, and with smoke filling the cockpit, he ordered the crew to bale out. No sooner had the order been given and the escape hatch opened, then the smoke appeared to subside, by which time, however, the rest of the crew had disappeared into the night. Robinson flew his Halifax home single-handedly without further incident and was awarded an immediate and thoroughly deserved DSO. The view of those who baled out is not recorded!

Another notable OC was Wing Commander James Tait. 'Willie' Tait was awarded the DSO on an incredible four occasions (as well as two DFCs), and some felt that he deserved a higher honour for his courage and leadership throughout the war. He was most famous for leading the successful raid to destroy the German 'Raider' that earned him the nickname 'Tirpitz' Tait. It was suggested that a Victoria Cross was denied him for joking with a senior naval commander that the sinking of the *Tirpitz* by the RAF had put the Royal Navy out of business![1]

When John and his compatriots arrived at the end of July 1944, Wing Commander Albert Markland was in charge, a man of no less stature and – remarkably – a wireless operator by trade. Markland was an excellent example of how war accelerates promotion, and true leadership is given a chance to flourish, regardless of initial rank, title or aircrew role. He was awarded his first medal for gallantry as a sergeant in August 1941 for a first tour of operations with 78 Squadron. Three years on, and as an acting wing commander DFC, DFM, he was now in charge of the squadron.

The Squadron moved around various airfields within the Group in the early years – Middleton St George, Croft, Linton-on-Ouse – before finally arresting at Breighton, by which time it had long since converted to the Halifax and was an established part of Harris's Main Force. Breighton had opened its doors for business as a satellite to Holme-on-Spalding-Moor at the very start of 1942, originally home to 460 Squadron of 1 Group before 4 Group's 78 Squadron moved in over the early summer of 1943. The station commander was Group Captain Hugh Brookes, a man with no experience of bomber operations who took it upon himself to fly with various crews and complete a tour, earning the DFC in the process.

In the twelve months prior to John's arrival, 78 Squadron had shouldered its fair share of bomber war, and its losses. Since June 1943, more than 600 men had been killed or were languishing in various prisoner of war camps in Germany. More than seventy had gone missing in a single month (August 1943) just as Bomber Command entered one of the most miserable and depressing periods in its history. Its commander-in-chief had vowed to smash the German capital from end to end, and hundreds of aircraft were lost in the attempt. The squadron lost five aircraft in one night (23 August) and three more less than a week later.

A particularly tragic loss was the death of Squadron Leader Peter Bunclark DFC DFM, the victim of a nightfighter. 'Bunny' Bunclark had risen through the ranks, winning the DFM for his tour with 76 Squadron as a sergeant pilot before being commissioned. He had survived a spectacular crash landing in July with his aircraft down to two engines, having first ordered his crew to bail out.

The loss of 30-year-old Squadron Leader Gordon Sells DFC one night in October was another tragedy. He had been a bank clerk before the war and exchanged a cash register for the controls of a heavy bomber. Sells was the 'B' Flight commander and on the sixth operation of his second tour. As well as the DFC he had also been mentioned in despatches.

Experienced officers seemed to be as much at risk as beginners. Flight Commanders and their deputies could not escape the chance shell bursting too close and causing fatal damage. Regular adjustments in height or direction could take them towards

danger and not away from it. Air gunners with fifteen or twenty
operations under their belts could still be caught unawares by a
nightfighter or sometimes two, working in pairs, the first as a
distraction and the second to deal the killer blow.

Flight Lieutenant Robert Shard, for example, had been a contemporary of John's in the desert in 1942, as an NCO pilot with 40 Squadron attacking targets in North Africa and Italy. He'd received a well-earned DFM after more than 250 hours of operational flying, and an immediate DFC two years later bringing his heavily damaged aircraft home from Magdeburg, ably supported by his flight engineer. He died on 16 February returning from Berlin. His aircraft ran out of fuel and he was obliged with his crew to bail out over the sea. There was only one survivor. Such were the odds.

March 1944 was another difficult month, and another in which more than seventy men were killed or captured. The nadir was the night of the 24th, a night during which the squadron lost five of its Halifax III aircraft, the worst casualties to be sustained by a unit thus equipped. Among the dead was Flight Lieutenant Donal Constable, an Australian skipper who had only recently been awarded a DFC for displaying 'fine fighting qualities', and whose, 'courage and coolness in the face of the enemy have been inspiring'. He was one of no fewer than 528 men 'missing' from that night's operations.

The casualty rate had dipped considerably since the end of the Battle of Berlin that concluded with the infamously disastrous attack on Nuremberg on 31 March. In what was the worst night for Bomber Command of the entire war, at least ninety-five aircraft were lost and many others damaged beyond repair and subsequently struck-off charge. In a night on which very few squadrons emerged unscathed, three crews were lost from Breighton. Among the dead was a 23-year-old Canadian flying officer, William Uyen, the only survivor from the crew of Robert Shard.

A kinder spring was followed by a troublesome early summer, with more than fifty men lost in June, the squadron losing four crews on the nights of 7-8 and a further three crews on 12. The former comprised an attack on the railway yards at Juvisy in support of the invasion, the latter to similar facilities in Amiens, putting paid to the lie that trips to Northern France were little more than a milk run for novice crews. In July, only two aircraft were lost, both while attacking flying bomb sites.

*   *   *

'Smithy' and his crew were quickly assimilated into squadron life. Such was the size of bomber squadrons that Flights were commanded by a squadron leader and squadrons, somewhat confusingly, were commanded by wing commanders. RAF stations were typically commanded by a group captain.

John's skipper assumed command of 'B' Flight to complement Squadron Leader Kentish as OC 'A' Flight and Squadron Leader Hurley as OC 'C' Flight. Jack Kentish had flown before the war, and been on the reserve. Frank Hurley, a Canadian born in Brandon, Manitoba, held a flying licence prior to the outbreak of war and had been with the squadron since October 1943. He was thus a veteran of the Battle of Berlin in the winter of 1943-44, and had also led a daylight raid on Noyelle in June that would later feature in the citation for his deserved DFC.

Operations were a far cry from John's days fighting in the Middle East. Now they were being undertaken on an industrial scale with carefully thought out plans and routes to target, and meaningful intelligence about enemy defences.

Harris and his staff officers in Bomber Command headquarters at High Wycombe decided the targets and gave them code words. Each city was named after a fish: Berlin was 'Whitebait'; Hamburg was 'Weaverfish'; Nuremberg was 'Grayling'. They also had code words for the type of attack: 'Goodwood' meant 'maximum effort'. Their wishes were then communicated to Group, and from Group to the individual squadrons in its command. Intelligence officers would first learn the basics – the target and how many aircraft were required. The detail would then follow: the bomb load; 'H' Hour; and then a host of other essential information including the method of attack and tactics to be deployed.

After the teleprinters had finished their mechanical chatter, the squadron would almost literally burst into life. There was much to be done. The IO and his team prepared the briefing, along with others such as the 'met' men, the engineering officer, and flying control team, all of who had their part to play. A Battle Order was posted, listing the captains and crews required for that night's operation, and giving times for the navigators' briefing and a main briefing, forty-five minutes later.

Crews would go out to where their Halifax was dispersed and check on the serviceability of their aircraft in close consultation with their groundcrew. If necessary, they would insist on a short air test. Nothing untoward – just a fifteen-minute check to ensure that all of the aircraft's systems, engines and controls were performing on the top line. Other specialist trades would arrive, including the 'sparks' responsible for the range of secret equipment that was now commonplace – equipment like 'Monica', 'Fishpond' and 'Boozer' that would help find fighters in the dark and H2S, a ground mapping radar technology that was little short of revolutionary for its time. Then came the petrol bowsers. And the bombs: cases of 4lb incendiaries; 500lbs; 1,000lbs; and, occasionally, a mighty 4,000lb blockbuster that had been so familiar to John in the desert. Some were intended to explode on impact or just above ground level and cause the maximum damage; others could be timed to go off hours and sometimes even days later, and catch the unsuspecting German rescue parties unawares. It was not pretty; it was terrible and total war.

In due course the main briefing would be held, the crews assembling for a great unveiling, and formal confirmation to the identity of a target that many had already guessed: limited fuel and maximum bomb load probably meant a short hop across the Channel; more fuel and fewer bombs, a long slog to Nuremberg, Berlin or even further. Stettin, perhaps, on the Baltic. None were popular. Berlin meant a minimum round trip of 1,200 miles; Stettin 1,260 miles. As the biggest port in the Baltic, and the main port for Berlin itself, it was a target of considerable importance. A red ribbon stretched across a map of northern Europe, with 'pools' of different colours to identify flak and searchlight concentrations and other points of interest along the route.

The IO talked through what he had learned about the target and its importance. Some cities were well known; others making their debut. The crews were told that all were important. He also provided information regarding bomber support operations. 'Intruders' would fly ahead of the bomber stream to confound and destroy the German defences, and if possible catch German nightfighters on the ground. Other friendly fighters would also be operating that night in a deadly game of cat and mouse with their German opponents, each desperate to 'see' the other first in the dark with their sophisticated radar. Crews were asked if they had any questions. Mostly they would ask about convoys; 'friendly' convoys had a habit of shooting first and asking questions later, and knowing their whereabouts for the return leg could be vital information.

Now they were winning the war, advancing and not retreating. The Allies had surprised the Germans by invading Northern France at

Normandy, rather than the Pas de Calais, and the Wehrmacht had been momentarily stunned. Now the Allies wanted to press home their advantage, to break out of Normandy and push the invaders back to the Rhine. To do so, however, required air support, and Harris – in deference to the Supreme Commander General Eisenhower – diverted his bombers from the task of bombing Germany's industrial heartlands to attack specific targets to support the Allies advance. Railways, fuel depots, ammunition dumps, troop and tank concentrations all became targets of opportunity, as well as ridding the menace of Germany's 'revenge' weapons, the V1 Doodlebugs and V2 Rockets that had started to rain from the sky over England and threatened yet another 'Blitz'. French towns and villages that John had never heard of became a regular feature in briefings, alongside now familiar German cities that promised a warm reception to anyone so bold as to venture their way.

Within a week of his arrival, John found himself on a Battle Order for the first time in almost exactly two years, 5 August. The target was La Foret de Nieppe, noted as a flying bomb storage facility that had already received the attention of RAF bombers on five previous occasions and perhaps highlighting the difficulties faced by heavy bombers in finding and destroying pinpoint targets. Now it was the chance of John and 78 Squadron to have a go.

Being a three-Flight squadron, and assuming all of its aircraft were available, 78 Squadron could contribute up to twenty-seven bombers to any particular raid and on this occasion twenty-five crews were briefed for the comparatively short hop to Flanders. 'Smithy' was earmarked a Halifax III (MZ320), a high performance, main production aircraft that used Bristol Hercules rather than Merlin engines to power it through the skies at speeds of up to 270 mph. A year or so before, losses of Halifax bombers had risen so alarmingly that its scope of operations had been limited; all that had changed with the Mk III, and by now – with Bomber Command at its peak strength – there were no fewer than twenty-six Halifax Squadrons in the line.

We got away shortly before 11.30hrs, 'Shep' Shepherd giving 'Smithy' a course to steer although, given that it was a daylight raid, it was more a case of 'follow my leader'. There were aircraft all around us. The Squadron aircraft were stepped at various heights for the attack, from between 14,000ft to 16,000ft and all armed with up to eighteen 500lb High-explosive (HE) bombs to ensure an optimum spread. Incendiaries were not required; there was nothing to burn. Instead we were relying on high explosive to create maximum destruction. It seemed to work.

On return, we were debriefed by the Intelligence Officer and his team. It was important that returning crews were spoken to while the raid was still fresh in their minds, and the detail was clear. Where had the bombs been dropped? From what height and at what speed? Had they seen any explosions? Did we hear the Master Bomber's voice clearly? Were the markers on time? What were the defences like? The flak? Had any fighters been seen? Or fighter flares? Had we seen any decoys or dummies? Had we seen any aircraft shot down and if so, where?

As well as wanting to confirm we had hit the right target, understanding more about where our aircraft had been shot down always seemed to be the part that the IO focused on the most. It allowed them to build a 'picture' of the raid. A report was needed by Group as quickly as possible to enable them to gauge the accuracy of the attack, to send their report to Bomber Command HQ, and whether more bombs were needed.

'Smithy' had found the target without difficulty, and listened intently to the instructions from the Master Bomber. For the past two years, and since the birth of Pathfinder Force, bombers had been guided to their targets by specialist squadrons and crews, and the aiming points marked with Target Indicators (Tis) designed specifically for the purpose. The man in charge of each raid was known simply as the Master Bomber who gave a running commentary to the Main Force of what was required, and whether they were bombing too short, too long, or too wide of the target, and correcting accordingly.

Isherwood, in the air bomber's compartment, had toggled his bombs away having visibly seen the target and been happy that his cargo had hit the storage site fair and square. The whole trip there and back had taken only three hours, a mere fraction of some of the raids to Berlin that could test an aircraft's endurance – and that of its crews – to the limit. Everyone, it seems, had been satisfied with the results, and agreed that the bombs had been well concentrated. Most satisfying of all was that all of the bombers had returned safely.

*   *   *

'Totalise' was the code word for an offensive by Allied troops of the First Canadian Army to break through the German defences south of Caen on the eastern flank and drive to capture the high ground north of Falaise. It was a bold plan whose ultimate objective was the collapse of the entire German front. It was a plan, also, that needed the support of the bomber boys.

The difficulty and dangers of bombing in front of Allied ground troops cannot be underestimated. When it went wrong, as it did on at least one occasion, it did so with tragic results. Pathfinders had to follow their leader's adage: that if they were not certain of the target, they were not to bomb. Frustrating though it was to return to base with their bombs still onboard, it was better than risk the accidental deaths of troops on the ground.

The first bombers left Breighton soon after 21.00hrs and headed for the assembly point. Again their bellies were bursting with high explosive, this time a mix of 1,000lb and 500lb bombs. Two hours into the operation, and with some of the squadron aircraft just starting their bombing run, the operation was abandoned. Not all of the aircraft received the instruction in time, although it appears no harm was done. Some opted to jettison their bombs over the sea; others like 'Smithy' (flying Halifax MZ311 and with a different air bomber, Flying Officer L Griffiths) brought them home. By 01.54hrs, all of the aircraft had returned safely to base.

Having abandoned their operation on 7 August, the crew only had to wait another two days before they were again on operations, this time to Dijon – 200 miles beyond Dreux, scene of John's first ever operation while still at OTU in 1941, a lifetime ago. The target on this occasion was a railway junction and yards, and a considerable amount of damage was achieved.

By now, a week after the Totalise campaign had begun, the Allied forces had advanced as far as they could go and a new plan was desired. 'Tractable', as it was known, would give them a second wind and finish what they had started. The plan was to close the Falaise 'gap', trapping the German soldiers inside, and so finish the Battle for Normandy. Once again it required the help of the bomber boys, who obliged on the first day of the attack (14 August) by committing more than 800 aircraft into the fray. All twenty-seven of 78 Squadron's Halifaxes took part, and all returned safely to base.

'Smithy', on his return, reported that the attack appeared to be 'excellent', and others seemed to agree. But not all the attacks achieved the results anticipated or desired by the commanders who planned them. One example of a good plan going badly wrong was an attack on German troop positions blocking the advance of the 3rd Canadian Division. There were seven aiming points, each marked by Oboe

Mosquitoes (Oboe was a blind bombing device that was incredibly accurate) and each with its own Master Bomber and Deputy. All went well until mid-way through the attack when a small number of Main Force aircraft dropped their bombs on a large quarry in which parts of the Canadian Forces were sheltered. They claimed to have bombed 'yellow markers'. Despite the best efforts of the Pathfinders directing the attack, and the constant remarking of the correct aiming points, a further group of bombers also dropped their explosives on the quarry, and in doing so killed thirteen men, injured another fifty-three, and destroyed a good many guns and vehicles.

John could not, of course, have had any idea of the tragedy that unfolded, not that the incident was hushed up. There were reasons why this unprecedented 'black' by Bomber Command occurred, but in the inquiry that followed, the Master Bombers (which included Wing Commander Thomas Bingham-Hall) were all exonerated. Bingham-Hall and his colleagues had done everything in their power to control where the bombs had fallen but their instruction had been – in part – ignored. The reason given for the mistake was the use by the Canadians of yellow flares to identify their position, and these had been taken to be the yellow Target Indicators used by the Pathfinders. In the 'fog of war' such mistakes are understandable, but scapegoats were needed, and a number of Pathfinders found themselves quietly posted away.

As if to illustrate how diverse the bombing war had become by the late summer of 1944, the target for the raid on 17 August was shipping and essential dry docks in the port area of Brest, with unconfirmed whispers that a German Pocket Battleship was in residence. Although by this stage of the war there were very few left, and those that still existed were skulking in far off fiords. John wondered how the defences at Brest would compare to the defences at Benghazi and decided not to think on it too hard. Neither filled him with any deep sense of joy.

In the event, the trip was largely uneventful. One pilot (Flying Officer Paul Christiansen RCAF – later DFC) returned early after an engine cut soon after take-off and, as for the rest, the raid was spoiled by heavy cloud, making the results difficult to observe. Two captains brought their bombs home.

A busy August for John ended with an attack on Homberg, a return in many respects to a 'traditional' Bomber Command target and historic for being the first major raid on the city in daylight since August 1941. On that occasion, ten out of the fifty-four aircraft had been shot down; this time it went in favour of the Allies, thanks in part to an escort of some nine squadrons of spitfires on the outward leg and seven on their return. Despite intense flak, all of the bombers emerged unscathed, save for a few holes. The Fischer-Tropsch synthetic oil plant was particularly hit.

John was flying with his regular crew. Also flying that day was Wing Commander John Young from 41 Base who was soon to assume command of the squadron from Markland.[2]

Casualties for the month had been comparatively light. Only two crews had failed to return: the crew of Warrant Officer Peter 'Gully' Gulevich RCAF on the night of August 12; and the crew of Flight Lieutenant Charles Howes RCAF on the twenty-fifth. Howes, a 22-year-old married man, was lost on operations to La Rochelle. He crashed on his return for reasons not fully explained. Gulevich and all of his crew were killed on an attack on Brunswick. His crew included an 18-year-old air gunner, one of the youngest airmen killed on operations that year.

Squadron life was by no means all work and no play. Whereas in the Middle East there had been little in the way of camaraderie and John had lived an insular existence, on a bomber station in 1944 it was completely different. The accommodation, for one thing, was much improved:

Breighton was a wartime station and we were accommodated in Nissan huts. Although they were not especially luxurious, they were certainly more comfortable than a tent and a hole in the ground. We also didn't have any scorpions to contend with and water and good food were in plentiful supply. As an officer, I had a room of my own, and on days when I wasn't on operations I would be woken by my batman at around 7.00am with a cup of tea. He would then take my shoes away to be cleaned, and asked if I needed any laundry doing. I usually went off for breakfast at around 8.00am, during which time he would tidy my room. When I had finished my ablutions I would make my way to the crewroom and report to the pilot.

There was also a life beyond the station:

We flew, ate and drank as a crew, each one depending on the other. We were, as many others have said before me, like a family, a unique bond that couldn't be broken. Perhaps, as nearly all of us were officers, it was different as we could mess together. But it was more than that. It was a different culture. More inclusive. We felt we belonged. We counted. We hadn't been forgotten.

Between us we bought an old Ford 8 car, and on occasions we were stood down, usually because of bad weather, we would fill the car up with 100-octane aviation fuel and head down, as a crew, to the nearest pub. (Later, when the CO heard about it, he made it clear that using aviation fuel was stealing and that we could be court martialled.)

There were four to choose from: the Bowman, the Swan, the New Inn and the Seven Sisters. Or sometimes we would drive into Goole or Selby, though I never got to York and the famous 'Betty's'. Because so many of our sorties were daylights, there was rarely the time. And anyway, our simple rule was that we would go to any pub that was open! The local pubs were very good to us. They knew we were operational crews and at closing time there was often a 'lock-in' and we'd stay for a few extra rounds.

Being married, I had different priorities of course. Some of the crew who were footloose and fancy-free wanted to chase the skirt, but I was happy just to talk and drink my pint. It was difficult too as being married and with a family, I had to make sure enough money was being sent home and had to look after my pennies, whereas the others always seemed to have money in their pockets.

Our biggest liability was our Canadian friend who despite being married was carrying on with some woman in Leeds. Apparently he was with her one night when her husband came home on leave and Shepherd was forced to bail out of the window. Of course he told us all when he got back and found the whole thing hilarious.

*   *   *

In September, Harris, who for the past few months had been subordinate to the needs of the Supreme Allied Commander, was released from his responsibilities – though not entirely. His command was pledged to continue supporting the ground offensive where required. As such the bomber crews found themselves briefed for yet another change in target.

The Battle for Normandy was effectively over, and Allied troops had marched triumphantly into Paris, the German garrison finally surrendering on August 25. Brussels was liberated soon after (on 3 September, the fifth anniversary of the war) and the Germans were in full retreat. But not everywhere. In certain quarters, German troops had obstinately dug in and refused to surrender. Pockets of resistance were left that seriously threatened the flow of fuel, ammunition and other essential supplies to the front line. Indeed the Allied advance, when it finally happened, almost happened too quickly and their supply lines were alarmingly over-stretched, so much so that Eisenhower – who had assumed control of Allied ground operations in northwest Europe from General Bernard Montgomery on 1 September – was obliged to order a halt.

While Cherbourg was in Allied hands, and providing a critical re-supply route, the Allies were in desperate need of further port facilities closer to the advancing armies. The Canadians were unable to capture the Channel ports quickly because Hitler had declared them Festungen (Fortresses) and the dock facilities that did fall into their hands had been largely destroyed. Montgomery captured Antwerp, but Antwerp was of little use without control of the Scheldt that remained resolutely in German hands. In the short term, these Festungen were simply ignored, but they could not be ignored forever. The ports – running from St Nazaire in the south to Dunkirk and the approaches to Antwerp in the north, contained more than 140,000 German troops, including crack troops of the Fallschirmjaeger (paratroopers).

One of these Festungen was Le Havre and for a period of seven days, Bomber Command undertook a series of heavy raids intended to dislodge the stubborn German defenders from their perch. Nearly 2,000 aircraft carried out these attacks and dropped more than 9,500 tons of bombs before their objective was finally met, and the garrison commander, Oberst Eberhard Wildermuth – a First World War veteran and holder of Germany's highest award for gallantry – willingly surrendered.

The most elaborate of all these attacks was on 10 September, when eight separate coastal batteries were earmarked for destruction, and each individual aiming point was given a codename and number after a make of car (Buick I and II, Alvis I to IV and Bentley I and II).

The significance in Pathfinding terms was that it effectively introduced a new lead player to an already distinguished cast – a 'Long Stop' – to control the whole attack. The man chosen for the task was the commanding officer of 582 Squadron, Wing Commander Peter Cribb DSO DFC, and his role was to cancel any inaccurate marking or bombing by dropping yellow TIs. The lessons of the previous month had been learned, and nobody wanted a repeat performance given the proximity of Allied troops. At one stage of the raid he was indeed obliged to intercede to show Main Force not to bomb beyond a particular point, and he also instructed the Master Bomber at one of the Buick targets to abandon his attack.

John's squadron contributed twenty-six aircraft in total in two separate attacks: seventeen in the early morning, and a further nine aircraft in the late afternoon. 'Smithy', in Halifax MZ320, took part in the morning raid, the bomb aimer easily being able to pick out the red target indicators and the aiming point through the smoke. Eleven thousand pounds of bombs rained down on the target from 8,000ft, causing untold damage.

Three more raids were completed that month on 12 September (to the synthetic oil plant at Scholven Buer in the northern outskirts of Gelsenkirchen), 20 September (to Calais as part of an offensive to liberate the port), and 25 September (another trip to Calais that was abandoned on the instructions from the Master Bomber). For the operation to Scholven Buer the crew had the squadron gunnery leader, Flight Lieutenant John Lane, in the mid-upper turret, though his exceptional skills were not required on the day. (Lane would later be awarded the DFC.)

The squadron lost two further crews in September: Flight Lieutenant Nelson Harding on the night of 15 September in a costly raid on Kiel; and 22-year-old Flying Officer John Swanson on the night of the twenty-third. Of the two crews, eleven men were killed, two taken prisoner and one evaded capture. Harding, whose body was never found and whose name is therefore commemorated on the Runnymede Memorial, had flown Blenheims with 23 Squadron during the Battle of Britain and was one of a small number of *The Few* who had later transferred to Bomber Command. He had only arrived on the squadron in July.

In comparison to other squadrons and at other times of the bombing war, such as the bloody Battles of Hamburg and Berlin, casualties had been manageable, albeit that every man lost was a tragedy to some. The availability of trained aircrew to replace them, however, was no longer an issue; a request was sent for new crew to [41 Base] and would arrive the next morning, either whole crews or 'spare bods' of particular trades to make up the numbers.

Perhaps inevitably, the squadron's fortunes took a turn for the worse on 6 October. The target was Gelsenkirchen, a relatively modest raid by Bomber Command standards comprising 320 aircraft, primarily Halifaxes of 4 Group targeting the oil plants at Sterkrade and Scholven Buer. Four Halifaxes failed to return; three were from 78 Squadron. It could have been more.

When the Form B arrived, it was to be a daylight attack on the Ruhr, the so-called 'Happy Valley' because there was nothing happy about it. Flak was thick, 88mm shells and heavier bursting at 18,000ft, each dirty black puff of smoke throwing red-hot shrapnel around the sky and hitting anything in its vicinity.

'Smithy' took off at 14.15hrs, one of the first to get away. The cockpit was unusually crowded. As well as the flight engineer, 'Smithy' also had a second pilot, Flight Sergeant Donald Phillips, alongside him, a novice New Zealander on a 'second dickey' trip. Every new pilot flew with a more experienced pilot first before being given command of his own crew on operations. That day Phillips was one of nine new pilots being 'blooded'. (Donald Philips went on to be commissioned and be awarded the DFC in May 1945 at the end of an eventful tour. His conduct throughout his operational tour was described as 'outstanding'.)

The trip out was uneventful until shortly after they crossed the enemy coast. Then disaster struck:

> *'Smithy' was leading the formation and as we crossed the coast, the skipper instructed me to go to the astrodome behind the cockpit and look out for fighters and other aircraft in the vicinity. Formation flying in daylight was something best left to the Americans! Steadily we gained height until we had reached our operational ceiling of about 20,000ft. We always preferred to get as high as we could so that the flak would focus its attention on those flying below and leave us alone.*
>
> *We were now part way across Holland en route to the target when the rear gunner came onto the intercom to say that two of our aircraft were getting closer and closer to our tail. 'Smithy' acknowledged the call and inched the throttles slightly forward to give us more speed.*
>
> *I am not sure precisely what happened next but I did see the result. Somehow the two aircraft that were gaining on us collided with one another and I saw them go down. It was terrible watching the two aircraft twisting and turning like sycamore leaves as they fell to the ground. I reported what I was seeing to the skipper and he told me to watch for parachutes. Sadly I didn't see anyone make it out.*[3]

'Smithy', in Halifax MZ391, proceeded to the target and dropped its eighteen 500-pounders from a height of 17,000ft, reporting later that a medium concentration of bombs could be seen falling on the target. They landed back at Breighton at 18.42.

At debriefing the news was indeed bad. Others had seen the collision and it appeared that at least two crews were missing. Then a third and a fourth crew failed to return, completing a very poor day in the office for the squadron. Although the crew of Flying Officer Edwin Love RCAF was later reported safe, having been damaged by flak and landed at the emergency field at Woodbridge, there was no news of the other three. Soon it would be known that all three would not return, and the twenty-two men on board were all dead.

The two aircraft that collided were flown by Flying Officer Raymond Stanley, aged 23, and Flying Officer Charles Crawford. Flying with Crawford that day was one of the second dickeys, Flying Officer Donald MacGregor RCAF, lost on his first operation with the squadron. The third Halifax to go missing was flown by Warrant Officer John Bradburn aged 22. It was believed that his aircraft was hit by flak. It was not a surprise:

> *We had been warned at briefing that there would be heavy flak over the target and so it proved. For the last 15 minutes or so of our run into the target, the flak came up thick and fast and burst all around. When we got back and talked to the other crews, we all agreed it had been 'hot'. The flak was radar predicted and they had quickly worked out our height and speed. Only two out of the 20 aircraft that left Breighton that night returned without damage.*

This poor run of luck continued the next day when another crew failed to return. Pilot Officer John Gillespie went missing following an attack on Kleve, being shot down near the battle area. John was not flying that day, having been given seven days leave.

*   *   *

Ops by now followed a similar pattern. The offensive against Hitler's oil was in full swing, the logic being that if you starved the enemy's aircraft and tanks of fuel, then you robbed them of their capacity to fight. It was much the same strategy that the Allies had pursued in the desert. The tactical bombing raids in support of the ground offensive were also giving way to other priorities, including on 14 October a sustained and unprecedented attack on the Ruhr.

The day before, Harris had received the directive for Operation *Hurricane*, to demonstrate the overwhelming superiority of the Allied Air Forces. The directive stated that the intention was to '…apply within the shortest practical period the maximum effort of the RAF Bomber Command and the VIIIth United States Bomber Command against objectives in the densely populated Ruhr…' What this meant in practical terms was two raids on the massive inland port or Duisberg within twenty-four hours; more than 2,000 Bomber Command aircraft alone were despatched during that period, dropping more than 7,500 tons of bombs. For its part, 78 Squadron put up twenty-six aircraft on the morning of the fourteenth, and a further twenty-three aircraft that night.

'Smithy' was again one of the first to take off for the earlier raid, with the bomb bay filled with nine 1,000-pounders and a handful of 500-pounders for good measure. All was going well until the bombing run. Isherwood was in the bomb aimer's compartment, his eye pressed against the bombsight, guiding his pilot to the target with a series of 'Left lefts', 'Rights' and 'Steadies' until the point of release:

> *The bomb aimer pressed his thumb down on the 'tit' and was at the point of calling 'bombs gone' when he realised that something was wrong. We had suffered what was known as a 'hang up' where a bomb or occasionally a whole load refused to dislodge. Discretion being the better part of valour, 'Smithy' decided to*

abandon the operation and head for an alternative target, in this
case Munchen Gladbach, where he hoped for better luck. And we
got it. This time, the bombs released on command, and we headed
for home.[4]

Happily, the squadron came through the onslaught without incident, save for five of the aircraft on the second raid being obliged to land away from base and one aircraft having to return early because of a faulty engine – something that would need to be explained to the commanding officer later in the day. Most squadron commanders were understanding of an early return, but didn't like them, and there would be an investigation. Aircraft and engines that were tired were prone to failure; ground crews who were tired could make mistakes. Pilots could also become war weary, and an early return could be a sign of a bigger problem, yet to unfold.

There was often a friendly rivalry among squadrons within a Group to be the best, and that included having the maximum number of aircraft on the top line when they were needed. It also meant delivering the best bombing performance, so much so that there was even a cup awarded each month to the squadron whose bombing photographs suggested the best results.

Any photograph that the IO could 'plot' (i.e. clearly identify on a map) was sent immediately to Group; if a crew obtained the ultimate prize – an aiming point photograph – then often the whole crew would be presented with a copy (with the operational details removed). A photographic 'ladder' was organised, with points awarded for bombing accuracy. For those unable to obtain a photograph at all, there was always an investigation. On some squadrons at certain times of the war there was a simple rule: no photograph; no operation. There were numerous reasons for a photographic failure, however, and not all of the blame rested with the crew.

Wing Commander Young was an 'old school' officer who led from the front. He had joined the RAF on a short service commission and been placed on the reserve as a flying officer in 1930. With war had come accelerated promotion, and 78 Squadron was his first wartime bomber command. Considerably older than many of the men under his command, he could get angry quite quickly, as John once found this cost:

> *The wing commander was quite a stout man, as I recall, and when he wasn't flying and we were operating, he would stand on the top of Flying Control and watch our departure. He was often there when we came back too.*
>
> *On one particular daylight, 'Smithy' was lining up the aircraft at the end of the runway, waiting for the 'Green' from the Aldis light in the chequered flight control caravan just to our left. As the aircraft in front took off and disappeared into the haze, the Green light 'blinked' and 'Smithy' pushed the throttles forward, assisted by the flight engineer to ensure that the levers did not slip back and lose vital power at the critical time.*
>
> *The torque generated by this huge surge of power, as I have mentioned previously, needed to be controlled by use of the rudders to keep the aircraft straight and level but on this occasion, the Halifax swung so suddenly and violently that we veered dangerously close to the control tower, causing the CO to jump back in alarm and fall off his feet. He was, as you can imagine, not very happy with us and told us on our return that he would 'have our garters for a necktie!'*

Happily, the wing commander did not carry out his threat.

* * *

The benign nature of the code word 'Gardening' hides a series of operations carried out by bomber command that were almost as dangerous as the 'Main Force' attacks that were now commonplace. 'Gardening' involved the 'planting' of mines, often (but not exclusively) in the North Sea and North Atlantic waters and channels but also rivers and canals to restrict the German shipping and naval routes, immobilise harbours and ports, and seriously impede the flow of shipping traffic to and from the industrial heartlands. To continue the gardening theme, mines were known as 'vegetables' and the target areas were given romantic names such as Nasturtiums, Hollyhocks and Jasmine.

In the early days, German sea-borne traffic included the transport of iron ore from Norway and Sweden, military supplies to support the campaign on the Russian front, and iron ore from Spain to the west coastal ports of France. Disrupting this flow of traffic involved dropping mines on a timed run using a visual pinpoint on the enemy coast and from a height of only 1,500ft. This left the crews and their aircraft incredibly vulnerable to light flak. Later, with the advent of H2S, mines could be dropped by parachute from a much safer height of several thousand feet, though this required considerable skill on behalf of the crew, and especially the bomb aimer, who had to calculate the strength of the wind and extent of the drift amongst other factors.

When Sweden refused to allow the passage of troops and materiel across her territory, the Norway-Baltic Sea passage through the Kattegat became a vital link, and of keen interest to The Admiralty, who were responsible for all sea mining whether carried out by aircraft, surface craft or submarine. It was to the Laeso Channel in the Kattegat – code-named 'Yew Tree' – that six 78 Squadron aircraft were detailed for the night of 15 October, including Halifax MZ391 with 'Smithy' at the controls. Between them they planted 23 MkIV vegetables as ordered. All returned safely to base.

*   *   *

Of all the 'Festungen', Antwerp was without doubt the most important. Although the port had now been captured, it was effectively useless while the Germans still controlled the Scheldt, and at the mouth of the Scheldt lay the island of Walcheren. The island was effectively in the shape of a saucer, with a rim comprising high sand dunes protecting a flat interior lying below sea level. An amphibious assault on the island was planned, but first it was necessary to breach the dyke at Westkappelle. This would allow the North Sea to pour in and flood the flat lands, neutralising the gun batteries and making it difficult for the Germans to move their troops into the battle area. Bomber Command was given the job of bursting the dyke.

It had several bites at what was to prove a particularly ripe cherry; between 3 October and 30 October, it made ten major assaults dropping around 9,000 tons of bombs. Shortly after, the troops moved in (with ample support from low level rocket firing Typhoons) and the island was captured.

Throughout the Walcheren 'campaign', 78 Squadron played its part. Unfortunately for our crew, however, detailed for operations on the penultimate raid, we suffered an early return. Not long after take-off, the aircraft (Halifax MZ391) started to vibrate as the starboard outer spluttered and then stopped. Unable to climb on only three engines, 'Smithy' ordered for the bombs to be jettisoned over the sea before returning to Breighton and landing without further incident. It was very disappointing.

On the night of 30 October, however, they had better luck for an attack on the historic city of Cologne, the third city of the German Reich. Cologne had been subjected to the first ever 1,000-bomber raid back in May 1942, when Harris launched his 'showpiece' attack to demonstrate the might of his bomber force. It had been hit dozens of times since, with a particular focus on its road and railway infrastructure. Two nights earlier the districts of Mulheim and Zollstock had been devastated by a force of more than 700 aircraft, but Harris was far from finished.

With their aircraft (MZ391) now repaired, they reached the target without incident. It was an unusual attack and a 'first' for John in that it featured a marking technique known as 'Wanganui'.[5] Pathfinders unable to mark the target on the ground would mark a point in the clouds through which the Main Force would aim their bombs. It was considered the least most favourable (and accurate) of all bombing techniques although on this occasion a considerable amount of damage was inflicted on the City's suburbs. Smithy was one of the first to return after a trip of almost six hours; two aircraft were obliged to abandon their attack because of engine trouble.

Chapter 7

Main Force

The winter of 1944-45 was especially harsh. For several weeks throughout November and December, the weather severely disrupted operations. Heavy cloud and squally showers gradually turned to snow, and for large periods the crews were stood down. At one point the airfield was covered in a 10inch blanket of snow, and drifts of up to 2ft were not uncommon.

When they did fly, poor visibility and freezing fog made conditions treacherous, and landing and taxiing accidents were not infrequent. Incidents of aircraft failing to take off or returning early through engine trouble also seemed to increase. One aircraft crashed near base while in the circuit attempting to land and another made an emergency landing at Woodbridge, the latter due to hydraulic failure robbing the pilot of brakes, flaps and other essential controls. Among the casualties in November was Flight Lieutenant Malcolm Buchanan, an Australian who had only recently been awarded the DFC for an action in which his flight engineer earned a Conspicuous Gallantry Medal (CGM) for outstanding heroism.[1]

With the snow falling heavily and no prospect of operations, ground crews, NCOs and even several officers lent a hand to clear the runways; hours of back-breaking work with a shovel and spade that had parallels with John's days 'out in the blue' in the Middle East, clearing the stones and rocks from the desert sand. Time would also be spent in the classroom, with lectures on all manner of subjects from the latest pathfinder and marking techniques through to escape and evasion. As one of the more senior aircrew, at least in terms of experience, John supported his Signals Leader where needed, teaching the tricks of the trade to those with less experience.

Even at this stage of the war, morale was a fragile commodity and could not be taken for granted. Operations that were briefed but then cancelled had a demoralising effect on the crews, especially those fast approaching the end of their tours. The poor weather also impacted the men's health, with a number of aircrew reporting sick with respiratory problems caused by cold, and compounded by the heights at which they flew. An outbreak of gastroenteritis added to their woes, perhaps the result of a damaged water supply, and there was even a case of scabies that led to one crew having to abandon its mission mid-flight.

There was a practical challenge in the mess too; the increasing volume of wartime commissions being granted to aircrew had led to considerable overcrowding. The number of officers had risen to 230 sharing a facility designed for only half that number. A request to extend the mess had been refused since the squadron would be soon reducing its Flights from three to two.

Christmas Day 1944 dawned to reveal heavy frosts and a thick ground mist that guaranteed there would be no flying that day, and the crews were allowed a few hours of respite to celebrate. An unfortunate dozen were called for operations the following day to St Vith, and all of them were obliged to land away at RAF East Fortune in Scotland. They flew back on the twenty-seventh.

There had been considerable movement among squadron personnel during the previous few weeks. Dozens of new crews had been posted in to replace those either killed on operations or who had done their bit and were due a hard-earned rest. Squadron Leader Kentish was posted on successful completion of his second tour and awarded an immediate DFC. Squadron Leader Hurley (who for a brief period had been squadron OC) also left Breighton. An experienced air gunner,

Flight Lieutenant Walter Smith (soon after appointed acting squadron leader), was posted in from 76 Squadron as OC 'C' Flight, and for a brief period, 'Smithy' assumed command of the squadron.

They also had a new station commander, Group Captain Ivoe Bird, who had replaced Group Captain Brookes in September[2].

By now, John was more than half way through his second tour of operations and in sight, once again, of a rest. The tour system had evolved during the war to arrive at a figure that satisfied the higher authorities but also gave the men of bomber command a sense of the achievable. In the early years, the survival rates had been miserable; now they were improving, but men needed a target, something to aim for to survive. For the bomber boys, a first tour was not to exceed 200 operational hours. Over time this had evolved into an equivalent figure of thirty operations, after which the crews would be rested and could be called back for a second tour of twenty operations. After this, they could not be called back again, remembering that every man was a volunteer. Despite this, some of those that did survive such remarkable odds did come back for a third and even a fourth tour of 'ops', and some went on to chalk up more than 100 bomber operations in their log books before finally calling it a day, or losing their lives to the inevitable. Squadron Leader Alec Cranswick DSO DFC, with whom John had flown in the Middle East, was a case in point.

As a flight commander and with one of the more experienced crews, 'Smithy' was entitled to his 'own' aircraft. He also had first choice of any new aircraft arriving on the squadron. The stresses and strains placed on the aircraft were considerable; battered airframes creaked noisily when in flight, and engines that had been flogged at thousands of revs for many thousands of miles eventually gave up. Corkscrew manoeuvres, steep banks and dives to avoid fighter attacks also pushed joints and mainplanes to the limit. Eventually they were 'retired', and passed down the line to the HCUs for the pilots to wring out the last of what feeble performance was still left before the scrap heap. Even new aircraft, however, did not necessarily guarantee a safe flight, as John recalls:

A brand new Halifax was delivered to us and as with all new aircraft, it had to be air tested. This involved a four-hour cross country trip to check out the handling of the aircraft and the functioning of the navigational aids, the radio and transmitter and the flight engineer's instrumentation.

'Smithy' decided to take her up and during the briefing by the met officer before we took off he warned us of cumulonimbus cloud near Peterborough. Cumulonimbus is a dense mass of cloud that usually forms in thunderstorms and can reach a height of 30,000ft. They can look very pretty, but if an aircraft spends any length of time in these clouds, ice can build up on the wings and fuselage and the instruments can freeze. The aircraft thus becomes unmanageable, stalls and descends out of control, even when flown by the most experienced pilots.

We took off and made height, climbing through the cloud to get above it and into clear sky. With the altimeter reading 20,000ft, we were still in cloud, and Smithy said that he would continue to climb until we were through it. No sooner had he called out our height than the aircraft appeared to stall and fall into a spin. The dive became faster and the spin more deadly, the centrifugal forces pinning me under my table.

'Smithy' was fighting a losing battle with the controls and ordered us to prepare to bail out. I tried to raise my right arm to unclip my parachute but could not move it. (Parachutes for everyone except the pilot were in two parts. The individual wore a harness to which the separate 'pack' had to be attached before baling out.) I just thought, 'well this is it' and waited for the end.

The altimeter showed we had fallen more than 18,000ft before 'Smithy' was at last able to regain control of the aircraft at around 2,000ft as the ice on the wings broke away, and the flying characteristics of the aircraft returned. It had been touch and go, and one of the only times I had been truly afraid.

We arrived back at Breighton and landed without further issue, grateful to be back on the ground in one piece. The following day the engineering officer reported that some of the wing bolts and engine mountings had been sheared off. The fuselage and tail fins were also twisted. The aircraft was declared a write off and I believe it was later scrapped.

*   *   *

For almost all of his operations, John flew with the same crew. Their first operation in the New Year was not until the night of 6 January when, in the company of more than 480 other Halifax, Lancaster and Mosquito aircraft, they set out to bomb Hanau, and an important railway intersection. Twenty-four aircraft from 78 Squadron took part, dropping high explosives and incendiaries, and all returned safely to base. One aircraft was badly damaged through enemy action.

On the night of 16 January, however, John was on the Battle Order as a 'spare bod', as wireless operator to Flying Officer Stanley Hubbard. Hubbard had only recently joined the squadron and had learned to fly in the United States.[3] There was no doubting his flying skills, and John was perfectly comfortable putting his life in the hands of an unknown quantity.

John had in fact asked for any spare bod operations available, for he was now in a hurry to complete his tour. Pressures from home, and in particular from his mother-in-law, were making life complicated:

The problem of flying with a flight commander or squadron commander is that they were limited in the number of operations they were allowed to fly every month. That meant we could go several weeks without operating and sometimes even longer, when the bad weather was taken into consideration.

Angela was pregnant again and my wife's mother had taken the rather unusual and hugely embarrassing step of writing to the squadron adjutant to say that I was not providing well enough for her financially. I was dumbfounded, both because it wasn't true but also that she had the nerve to write such a letter when I was risking my life for King and Country. It was a very spiteful thing of her to do and showed a total lack of awareness of the dangers we faced every time we went on operations.

The letter did have an impact on me, however, and that was that I wanted to finish my tour as quickly as possible so I could be with my wife and get her away from her mother's poisoning influence. In the event only one trip was ever made available to me and that was my longest flight ever.

Their target was Magdeburg, a thousand-year old city that was no stranger to conflict and brutality, having been besieged in the Thirty Years War and seen two out of every three of its inhabitants slaughtered. Situated at a natural crossroads on the Elbe, it had recovered to become a major inland port, linked to the Rhine by the Mittelland Canal and to Berlin by a series of smaller waterways. Indeed on completion of the Mittelland Canal in 1937, Magdeburg became the centre of a 7,000 mile network of inland waterways extending from the Rhine to East Prussia.

As well as the canals and waterways, the city was also at the junction of a number of major roads and railway lines. Huge ironworks (the Grusenwerke, a branch of the mighty Krupp) produced millions of tons of armour and machinery, and smaller plants manufactured instruments, cement, chemicals, glass, rubber ware and even artificial manure. As well as heavy industry, Magdeburg was also critical to the production of sugar and chicory. No surprise, therefore, that it was a favourite target of bomber command and had been since 1940.

On that particular night, the planners had only one intention: to flatten what they could of the city by area bombing – not only the industrial and manufacturing sites, but also the homes of the workers without whom nothing could be made. Aircraft were loaded with a mix of 2,000-pounders and incendiaries, the heavy bombs to blow the roofs from the buildings and the incendiaries to set fire to what was left standing and inflict maximum damage and terror. There was perhaps some justification for why Goebbels, Germany's Propaganda Minister, referred to bomber command aircrew as 'Terrorfliegers'; less so for calling them gangsters.

The bulk of the force was made up of Halifax aircraft from 4 and 6 Groups, 78 Squadron contributing twenty-three bombers to the fray. For once, the weather over the target was clear, and the red target indicators dropped by the attendant 8 Group Pathfinders were also easy to see. Hubbard's bomb aimer had no difficulty toggling away his bombs and had the satisfaction of seeing several explosions below to add to the extensive fires that had already started. Everything about the attack indicated a successful raid and so it proved. The raid devastated more than forty per cent of the city, with an estimated death toll of more than 15,000 inhabitants.

The bomber force did not have it all its own way, however. While all of the 78 Squadron aircraft returned home (one returned early having been obliged to abandon his attack), some seventeen Halifaxes were shot down, including four from one of the 6 Group Squadrons and a number of casualties among the Free French.

*   *   *

Within a Bomber Command Halifax, every member of the crew had a vital role to play to ensure not only their operational effectiveness but also their very survival. Some – and notably the pilot, navigator and air bomber (abbreviated to a category known as PNB) – would have spent more than two years of training, usually in establishments overseas. Flying training and air navigation schools had been established all over the British Empire and former Colonies, from the United States to South Africa, out of harm's way, in theory. Training for the 'trades' – the flight engineers, wireless operators and air gunners – was somewhat more truncated, and could be carried out closer to home at dedicated wireless and air gunnery schools, often in some of the less hospitable parts of the country, near the coast.

The captain of the aircraft was almost always the pilot, regardless of rank. He was the prime decision maker with ultimate responsibility for the safety of his crew. He worked closely with the navigator, probably the most important of all crew positions, without whom the target might never be found. The navigator in turn worked closely with the air bomber and wireless operator as part of a team.

Training for air bombers included basic navigation and air gunnery skills; in good visibility and at low level in particular, an air bomber would identify landmarks for the navigator to confirm his position. The wireless operator, meanwhile, would listen out for updates regarding wind speeds and weather fronts that could have a dramatic impact on an aircraft's position and progress. When not at his station, and particularly over the target, he would also be asked to act as an extra pair of eyes and ears for the gunners, keeping a sharp look-out for night fighters and other aircraft that might be lurking in the dark.

After assisting the pilot with take-off, the flight engineer would maintain a watching brief over the aircraft's systems and instruments, most notably the engines, monitoring temperatures, oil and fuel consumption. A Halifax could burn off one gallon of high-octane fuel per mile; making sure there was sufficient to get home after a trip of eight or nine hours required concentration and skill.

For the air gunners, there was never time to relax. A bomber could receive the unwelcome attention of a fighter at any moment during an operation, and not just over enemy territory. The German nightfighters were known to pursue bomber streams until they were well out into the North Sea, explaining why so many aircraft disappeared without trace. They were also known to loiter around UK airfields, hoping to catch tired crews unawares, when they thought they were safe.

In every operational flight you had to be alert and keep your wits about you. I had set routines of course: every thirty minutes I would listen out for transmissions from Group on an agreed frequency. The information could be vital: wind speeds; weather over the target; weather at home over base; diversions. You certainly could not risk missing a transmission. It was information that could save your life. If you missed a recall, for example, you could find yourself battling your way to the target as the only aircraft in the sky! It happened to others on more than one occasion.

There was never any time to be bored or frightened. There was too much to do, and when over the target I would help spot flak and fighters.

Although occasionally apprehensive before a flight, John was never particularly frightened. He believes this had something to do with his upbringing:

I was often aware of things going on around me but not part of it, as for example with the mutiny in the desert. I was like a disinterested bystander. It was the same with fear. I was aware of LMF – the dreaded 'Lack of Moral Fibre' that was a stamp of shame for cowards – and I had heard stories of how some men had been treated, with their badges of rank stripped from their sleeves and being demoted in the ranks. There were the two sergeants in the Middle East who had 'forfeited their commanding officer's confidence'. But for some reason I could never understand why people became so frightened and couldn't go on. It was somehow alien to me. It is difficult to explain.

Perhaps my detachment was because of my youth. From the age of 16 I had been obliged to fend for myself, without help from others. That had made me very self-resilient and also old beyond my years. I never had to rely on support from anyone else, other than when we were flying. That was different. Then you were part of a team, and the team was only as strong as the weakest member. So you made sure it was never you.

If I were afraid of anything then it was how I would die. Would I be blown to pieces or burn to death? Would I be trapped in the aircraft by centrifugal forces, fully conscious and waiting for the impact? I hoped, as I think we all did, that if we did have to die, it would be quick and we'd know nothing about it. The Halifax had a better survivability rate than the Lancaster but it was never discussed. No-one ever thought they would die.

Whenever we flew, I applied 100 per cent concentration to our operation. You had to. Your life and the lives of the crew could depend on it. That is why it never bothered me flying as a spare bod; I had my job to do and would ensure I did it to the best of my ability. I trusted that others would be doing the same.

John's first action on entering the aircraft was to make his way to the wireless operator's position and switch on the Identification Friend or

Foe (IFF) – an electronic 'identifier' to prevent the aircraft from being shot down by friendly fire. He would then enter the action in his log and open the 'watch'. An abundance of paperwork would include the Q Signals book to support virtually every navigational requirement: QDM – a signal to request the correct magnetic course to steer for base; QDH – a signal for the safe descent through cloud:

> *You asked the pilot for permission first before making the request.*
> *Then you would clamp down the Morse key until they could*
> *effectively 'find' you, when they would then transmit the height*
> *and course to steer that would bring us over our airfield and the*
> *approach to our runway. It was essential that you could do this*
> *and that you could do it right in an emergency.*

When the aircraft crossed the enemy coast, John had another role: to drop 'Window'; a simple yet incredibly effective way of confounding the enemy defences:

> *Window comprised thin strips of aluminium that we released in*
> *bundles down the flare chute, two bundles every minute, so that*
> *they created metallic 'clouds' in the sky. As they fell they would*
> *play havoc with the German radar, giving the impression that*
> *there were many thousands of us when sometimes there might only*
> *be a comparatively small number. They also made it virtually*
> *impossible for the German controllers to guide their nightfighters*
> *with any degree of accuracy.*

Besides his Marconi T1154 Transmitter and R1155 Receiver, John also had responsibility for 'Fishpond', a fighter-warning device that formed part of the H2S installation. A 'blip' on the screen might indicate a fighter closing in from the stern. But for every measure there was a counter-measure, and the device that was designed to protect could in fact be an aircraft's Achilles heel.

Certainly the German night fighter force was still a menace. A tiger is at its most dangerous when wounded, and the German pilots had been badly mauled. The huge increase in raids, mounted by both Bomber Command and their American counterparts, were taking their toll in a war of attrition that the Luftwaffe could no longer hope to win. It was being starved: starved of pilots; starved of landing grounds; starved of fuel. The Allied advance had robbed them of their early warning stations on the coast, and so they had less time to prepare or predict the bombers' intentions. While the number of fighter aircraft and pilots had in fact increased between July – November 1944, the operational effectiveness of the Nachtjagd had declined. Nominally, Germany's nightfighter squadrons were in rude health; in reality they were slowly bleeding to death.[4]

And the hunters were themselves now being hunted by radar equipped Mosquitos, against which they had little defence beyond their wits. Several of the nightfighter arm's most experienced leaders (the top 'aces' were known as 'Experten') were killed during the winter of 1944-45; among them, the Staffel Kapitan (squadron commander) of 9./NJG1 and Hauptman Heinz Struning, an ace with some fifty-six 'kills', shot down by a Mosquito. Such men were impossible to replace.

While the night fighters were undoubtedly losing their potency, they were still scoring kills: in January and February 1945, Nachtjagd crews flew more than 1,800 sorties and claimed almost 300 victories. But they lost almost 100 of their own aircraft, and the majority of crews flying them. It was not just the nightfighters that the Bomber Command crews had to deal with. With daylight raids becoming increasingly commonplace, they now had to contend with the Luftwaffe's day fighters, single-engined Messerschmitt Bf109s and Focke Wulf

FW190s that could still pack a punch in the hands of an experienced pilot.

The air gunners were familiar with single and twin-engined piston aircraft. Messerschmitt Bf110s, 410s, Junkers 88s, and even the occasional Heinkel He 219, though fortunately they were few and far between. They had seen enough of them in their time, and the darkened silhouettes in the crewroom were a constant reminder should their recognition skills need sharpening. But now they were also beginning to report a new adversary as some of the Luftwaffe's 'secret' weapons were thrown into the fray.

On the night of 14 February on a raid on Chemnitz, one of the squadron's aircraft – flying on three engines – was attacked no fewer than four times by a Junkers 88, but the fighter did not have it all its own way. The Halifax gunners returned fire and on the third attack reported that the enemy's port wing was aglow. The Junkers broke away during the fourth attack with the port wing on fire. The crew considered the enemy 'probably destroyed'. On the same night and on the same raid, another Halifax was attacked by what the gunners identified as a Messerschmitt Me262, a new jet fighter that was being pressed into service by day and by night. Both gunners opened fire and, despite the Messerschmitt's incredible speed, they got lucky. The enemy aircraft was seen to burst into flames and explode on the ground. They did not have long to congratulate themselves before being set upon by another fighter that they again identified as being 'jet-propelled'. This time, however, the combat was inconclusive.

It had been a busy and difficult night for the Squadron, and several aircraft returned with battle damage, among them Flight Lieutenant J. Davidson. His Halifax had been badly shot about on the way to the target and he diverted to Manston on his return. The Halifax (MZ791) never flew again.

As well as the raid on Chemnitz, four Halifax were despatched on Gardening duties and one failed to return. Flight Lieutenant Raymond Cumming and his experienced crew were lost without trace. His flight engineer John Rice was only nineteen.

John's own experience of nightfighters was particularly fortunate:

> *Our gunners were always on the lookout, traversing the sky in their turrets in a search pattern so that we would not be caught unawares. German night fighters would usually attempt to sneak up on you from below and behind, where they were difficult to see.*
>
> *Our 'secret' weapon was 'Fishpond', which could detect if an aircraft was approaching. (It was much better than 'Monica'. Monica was an audible warning that was hugely unreliable and used to sound off all the time.) The skill with Fishpond was in identifying whether the 'blip' on the cathode screen was an enemy fighter, or one of our own aircraft flying a little too close. This was relatively easy to recognise with practice: if it were another bomber, the blip would move little as we were all flying at approximately the same speed. If the spot of light was moving quickly, at overtaking speed, then it was likely to be a fighter.*
>
> *On one night I had a clear warning of trouble. A blip appeared on the screen at a range of about 4,000yds. I watched it closing quickly to around 2,000yds at which point I warned the skipper to corkscrew to port. 'Smithy' then flung the aircraft into a series of left-handed dives and turns in a corkscrew motion and the fighter was lost. Although we would occasionally be splattered by flak, this was the only occasion we were intercepted by a fighter. Compared to many others in the squadron, we seemed to live a charmed life.*

The crew's next operation came three nights later during an attack on Wesel. Although not one of the better-known German towns, Wesel, on the east bank of the Rhine, was strategically important, ahead of the Allied advance towards the mighty river. As such it was singled out for four major attacks on 16, 17, 18 and 19 February.

Wing Commander Young led the Squadron for the daylight raid on the seventeenth, in the company of eighteen of his crews. Three Groups were involved in the attack with the bulk of the force made up of 4 and 6 Group. (4 Group now had a new commander, Roddy Carr having been replaced by Air Vice Marshal John Whitley in a move by Harris to give some of his senior men wartime command). They arrived over the target to find the town covered under a blanket of thick cloud and almost immediately the Master Bomber instructed the Main Force pilots to abandon the operation and return home. Not everyone heard the broadcast in time, however, including 'Smithy' in M-Mother, who dropped his high explosive having identified the target using Gee and headed for home.

> *The journey home was long and slow as we were down to three engines, our port outer having developed a fault. This was always a nervous time. The flight engineer was busy re-directing the fuel to the three 'good' engines and keeping a careful watch to make sure none of them overheated. The real problem however, was the weather; we were in thick cloud almost all the way there and all of the way back. We were diverted to North Pickenham,[5] a USAAF base in Norfolk, where we landed with our prop feathered. 'Smithy' pulled off an excellent landing and we were entertained for the evening by our American friends while our aircraft was repaired. We flew back to Breighton the following morning.*

The raid had been something of a disappointment for all concerned and most disruptive, with the squadron's aircraft scattered all over the

UK. A large number had made for Tuddenham, one of several airfields equipped with a primitive fog dispersal system known as FIDO. Others landed at Mildenhall, Carnaby and Manston. Only four of the nineteen aircraft that got away landed back at base.

* * *

The German's defence against the bomber streams was not limited to flak or fighters. They were also ingenious inventors, developing huge 'decoys' to lure the unsuspecting airmen away from the 'genuine' targets, such that their bombs fell harmlessly into the surrounding countryside. They tried to use this tactic to defend the Reisholz district of Dusseldorf, home to the Rhenania Ossage refinery, on the night of 21 February but it failed spectacularly. Oil production was halted permanently.

John was somewhat frustratingly stood down for the Squadron's attacks on Worms and Essen, when again the nightfighters were busy. Worms was a new target to the men of Bomber Command. It was an area raid that knocked down or damaged two out of every three buildings and displaced more than half of the population. The raid on Essen was once more in daylight, and some must have wondered whether there was still anything left of the Krupps Steel works to bomb. Even the heavy flak, that had once been a permanent feature of the Ruhr, seemed to have lost its intensity.

Kamen was the next on the list, a few minutes flying time to the east of Dortmund, and specifically the synthetic oil plant in Bergkamen to the north of the town. They were virtually unopposed. Only one aircraft was shot down out of an attacking force of 340 bombers, such was the Allied air superiority at this time. (Losses had long since been reported as percentages.) The aircraft was a Halifax from 415 Squadron, the unfortunate pilot being a Canadian, Warrant Officer Lewis Russell:

We all saw the Halifax shot down. There must have been at least a hundred pairs of eyes watching the Halifax as it fell, in flames, over the target. Although there were no fighters about, there was some heavy flak and clearly it had registered a direct hit. It was a sickening sight to see it go down and not be able to do anything about it. There were no parachutes and no survivors. While I had of course become accustomed to seeing aircraft shot down, and the empty tables at the post-op meal, it was still difficult to watch.

February had been relatively kind to the squadron in terms of casualties: only two aircraft were missing. As well as Raymond Cummings who had gone missing while Gardening in Rostock on the Baltic Sea coast, one of the RNZAF pilots, 24-year-old Flying Officer James Gutzewitz, was shot down and killed at the start of the month. Three of his crew survived to become prisoners of war. They were the last aircraft to be lost during John's time on the Squadron.

Whenever a crew went missing, and it was clear that they had not made an emergency landing elsewhere, a telegram was despatched to the next of kin followed by a personal letter from the commanding officer. This usually happened the next day. These letters often held out some hope that an individual who was missing might later turn up safe as a prisoner of war. In more than 55,000 cases throughout the war, however, there was no such good news. Bomber Command's losses were terrible.

While the telegrams and letters were being sent, there was the practical issue of what to do with the missing airman's kit. It was also important to clear his bed for the next man to occupy. For that purpose, a Committee of Adjustment was established and an officer appointed to go through the missing man's personal effects.

*Sometimes this task fell to me, and if they were married men then
I would remove anything that might cause further embarrassment
or distress to the widow. One married man also had a girlfriend
on the base, and I saw to it that any incriminating evidence such
as letters or photographs were destroyed.*

Having now flown twenty operations from Breighton, John was
coming to the end of his second tour. He was tired and he didn't mind
admitting it. Added to his first tour in the Middle East, he had now
survived more than 400 operational hours and was living on borrowed
time. At one point of the bomber war, it had been calculated that your
chances of surviving a first tour were no better than one in four; the
odds lengthened for surviving a second. Experience was no guarantee
of survival. Indeed many aircrew coming back from a 'rest' at OTU
went missing on one of the first operations of their second tour, partly
because tactics and the dangers had changed. John had been lucky and
was now in sight of home. He could not be obliged to fly a third, but
then the war would be over soon anyway.

The RAF hit Essen for the last time on 11 March and celebrated
by sending out the largest force ever to attack a single target. The
Squadron itself celebrated by committing twenty-two aircraft and
their commanding officer to the project, joining 1,057 other aircraft in
the late afternoon for the short trip to the Ruhr. They arrived only to
find the target once again totally obscured by cloud, although this had
been considered in the plan, for Oboe-equipped Mosquitos were on
hand to mark the aiming point. The Master Bomber (call-sign 'Hooky')
was clear in his instructions, and this time 'Smithy' had no trouble
in following orders or seeing the smoke puffs that marked where to
bomb. The crew was somewhat depleted, the gunners' positions being
taken by Flying Officer Gregg and Flying Officer Nichol. John was
also flying with a spare bod flight engineer, albeit a senior one: Flight

Lieutenant Walker. Littler had been poached by the wingco. John need not have worried. The operation passed off without incident, although they could not see what damage their eighteen 500lb bombs had caused. Only at debriefing was it clear that the raid had been a complete success. It all-but paralysed production until the American land forces arrived soon after. Before the attack, one well-known Pathfinder air bomber had remarked that there could not have been much left in Essen to bomb. Now it was in total ruins.

Even so, three Lancasters were lost on the raid; there was only one survivor from the three crews. John, along with several others, reported a phenomenon known as 'scarecrows' over the target. 'Scarecrows' were thought to be a rocket-like projectile that could reach the bomber stream and explode with tremendous force, bringing down anything that was within range. In fact there was no such thing; what John and the others had seen were their own aircraft exploding, hit by heavy flak and spraying their fiery remains across the evening sky.

Two days later, John's name was on the Battle Order for what would be his last operation with 78 Squadron, and his last operation of the war. He did not know that at the time, however.

At briefing, the target was revealed as Wuppertal. It held no fear; John had never heard of it. It was, he learned, 40km to the east of Dusseldorf and at the heart of Germany's chemical production. It was said to be where a new glue was being developed to help with the construction of the Nazi's new aircraft programme. Wood was still in plentiful supply, and was the preferred material for a new generation of weapon. So it was to be yet another trip to the Ruhr in daylight, which always brought different dangers, and the wing commander was coming with them, which meant it was unlikely to be easy. Commanding officers and flight commanders were supposed to limit the number of operations they were allowed to fly each month and so tended to choose the more difficult, to lead by example. This was the third occasion that Bomber Command had been briefed for Germany's 'Black Country' in as many days.

John donned his flying gear, unaware that he was doing so for the last time:

> *The wireless operator occupied one of the warmest positions in the Halifax and I dressed accordingly. Over my blue serge battledress I wore the traditional and much-prized sheepskin jacket and matching sheepskin flying boots. I had shunned the more modern version in two parts, with a top half that was designed to detach to leave what looked like a normal shoe. It was meant to help with escape and evasion but I didn't see the need for it. In the desert I wore goggles; you had to because of the sand. In Europe there was no need. You simply wore a leather flying helmet with integrated headphones.*

There was the usual chatter on the truck as it dropped various crews off at their respective dispersals. 'Chiefy', their groundcrew boss was there to greet them and to assure the pilot that all was well. The engines were performing on the top line and the issue with the mag drop had been resolved. A few patches of fabric had been painted over where flak splinters had left their mark, but otherwise the aircraft – Halifax MZ391 – looked as good as new. John wandered around to the tail wheel for the customary good-luck pee before clambering on board. He was not one for lucky mascots, but there were certain rituals that had to be followed.

Shortly after 12.45 in the afternoon, the first of the heavy bombers threaded their way from dispersal to the end of the runway, and patiently waited their turn and a green light from the chequered van. Then with the brakes released and the throttle levers fully forward, the first of the aircraft grumbled and groaned its way into the sky as another took its place. The CO stood with a small party of WAAFS to wave the men on their way. It was a tradition. And it was appreciated, although on some squadrons, and to the hottest targets, it was appreciated more if their squadron commander was with them!

Halifax MZ391 took off at 12.52 and reached the target a little more than three hours later. At 16.00hrs precisely, the bomber aimer toggled away the bombs on the blue smoke puffs dropped by the Pathfinders and checked his computer to ensure there were no hang-ups. The Halifax continued flying straight and level for a further few moments to allow the camera to take its essential photograph, then the bomb doors were closed, the throttles thrust forward, and the aircraft headed for home, relieved of its load of 250- and 500lb bombs.

As they headed for home, a strange shape was spotted in the sky moving at incredible speed, so fast that the rear and mid-upper turrets could not traverse their guns quickly enough to draw a bead, so small that it was almost imperceptible. Its only identifier was a thin plume of smoke that drew a straight, near-vertical line in the watery-blue sky. It was another of the Fuhrer's 'miracle weapons', a Messerschmitt Me163 Rocket fighter, appropriately named 'the Komet'. It was capable of speeds in excess of 600mph but had a range of just twenty-five miles and could only remain in the air for a few minutes before gliding back down to earth. An exciting idea on paper, in practice the pilot had only moments to identify a target, sight his guns and fire before he was passed. Despite this the Komet posed far less of a threat than the Germans had envisaged, but it gave the crews something new to speak about at the post-op interrogation.

The crew landed at 18.10hrs, and as the engines shut down, John switched off the transmitter/receiver and the IFF then entered the action into his log. Waiting for the crew bus to take them back for debriefing, there was that moment they had all come to treasure, a brief moment of peace. For more than five hours their senses had been bombarded with constant noise, and it took a little while to re-acclimatise to the quiet all around. A quiet that shouted loudly that they were alive.

In his billet less than an hour later, the interrogation over and with his post-op meal of bacon and eggs eaten, John relaxed on his bed and paused to reflect. He took out his faded blue observer's and air gunner's log book from the top drawer of his bedside table to write the details of the day's operations. The format was always the same: date; hour; aircraft type and number; pilot; duty; and remarks, including the results of any bombing or gunnery. On the right hand side was a column for flying time, and the time carried forward. The entry was written in green ink to denote a daylight raid.

> *'Smithy' came to see me and told me I'd done enough. That it was over; I had completed my second tour. I had very mixed emotions, but I was far from euphoric. If anything I felt a little deflated. While I was on ops, all you could think about was surviving and doing your job to the best of your ability. All of the concerns I had for my wife and my family had to be pushed to one side. You could not afford to be distracted. Being taken off ops felt like I was exchanging one set of problems for another.*

John remained on the station for almost three weeks before being formally posted to 11 OTU on 7 April 1945. It gave him time to say goodbye to his skipper and the rest of the crew, 'Smithy' being promoted to wing commander and posted to command 102 Squadron. It also gave the OC 78 Squadron time to complete another Confidential Report, this one considerably more flattering than the last:

This officer has completed two operational tours and has proved himself to be a very efficient instructor on Signals duties. He can be relied upon in any circumstances.

Group Captain Bird, in his role as station commander, concurred. He wrote: 'A reliable member of aircrew and a useful officer.'

The war in Europe was fast drawing to a close.

Chapter 8

Final Approach

Bomber Command and the RAF in general had increased significantly in size in the six years of war. To the ranks of the regular air force had been added thousands of irregular aircrew, some of whom had excelled in wartime service, many of whom couldn't wait to leave. With the formal surrender of the German armed forces on 8 May, however, came the problem of what to do with them all.

After leaving Breighton I was posted to 11 OTU at RAF Westcott in Buckinghamshire which was used as a clearing centre for Allied prisoners of war being repatriated back to the UK by air in Dakotas and Lancasters as part of 'Operation Exodus'. It was here that I met up once again with Joe Brookes and between us we helped to process the returning prisoners, some of who had been 'in the bag' for five years since Dunkirk.

The operation, which started on 2 April and went on until 3 June 1945 saw 75,000 personnel airlifted back from Europe with around 35,000 landing at Westcott:

The soldiers entered one end of the hangar (which had been decorated with bunting) where they were deloused and issued with new kit before they reached us. We took their particulars and escorted them on to transports where they were conveyed to army reception camps. Despite the difficult conditions that some

*of them had to confront, they all seemed to be reasonably healthy
and very happy to be home.*

In the meantime, John had decided to apply for a permanent
commission, his application being signed by his former squadron and
station commanders. Their recommendation was endorsed by the
AOC 4 Group who wrote:

> *From my knowledge of the senior assessing officer and the station
> commander, and taking into account the assessments and remarks
> recorded by them, I consider Flying Officer Brennan to be suitable
> for consideration for appointment to a permanent commission.*

With his future in the RAF secured, the powers that be decided that
John needed to be inculcated more into the machinations of a peacetime
service, and as such he was posted to RAF Credenhill in Hereford
on an administration course. Credenhill was a non-flying station used
almost exclusively for training, and it was here that John was given the
basic skills he would need to become a station adjutant.

Having taken and passed the necessary exams, John embarked on a
new 'career', initially being posted to 5156 Mechanical and Electrical
Squadron, an airfield construction unit.

> *At the beginning of August, we were informed that we were being
> posted overseas to the island of Okinawa, the nearest Island to
> Japan. We were to construct airfields for the final assault. While
> the war in Europe was over, the Japanese were still holding out in
> the Pacific. On our way to Southampton, however, the first of the
> atom bombs was dropped on Hiroshima, and when we arrived we
> were instructed to return to our base. A short time later the war*

ended, the squadron was disbanded, and I was posted to RAF
Methwold in Norfolk.

At Methwold, John settled quickly into the station routine, learning
from those around him. After the excitement of operations, the
work was mundane, perhaps even boring. As assistant adjutant, he
was responsible for all forms of discipline, minor breaches that did
not require the attention of the commanding officer. He missed the
camaraderie of squadron life and was reminded of what he'd left
behind in September 1945 when he received a phone call from his
former skipper:

'Smithy' 'phoned me and asked me if I'd seen the latest edition
of the London Gazette. I hadn't, of course, so he told me I'd
been awarded the Distinguished Flying Cross. 'You deserved it
Paddy', he said, and I realised that he'd been the one who'd made
the recommendation.

Confirmation of John's DFC appeared in a supplement to the London
Gazette dated 21 September, 1945. The name appearing immediately
below his was none other than Joseph Edmund Brookes. Although there
was no citation beyond the 'usual' mention of displaying 'fortitude,
courage and devotion to duty', John was credited with sixty-three
sorties, and a total of 112 flying hours. For some reason, the 296 hours
accrued in the Middle East had disappeared!

Despite being something of a fish out of water, John made a good
early impression with his immediate superiors at Methwold. Squadron
Leader Love, and the AOC 3 Group, Air Commodore Frank Nuttall,
believed that he would make a sound administrative officer with further
experience. Experience, however, appeared to be John's Achilles heel,
and others were less generous with their appraisals, one describing

him as having 'an operational aircrew attitude to things in general' and even to 'antagonise those with whom he has to work'.

Nine months at Methwold was followed by a posting to RAF Wyton, John arriving as a recently promoted flight lieutenant to assume duties as station adjutant. Squadron Leader William Pearce Harvey, unsurprisingly a regular air force officer, effectively damned John with faint praise in his confidential report: 'This officer has an unfortunate manner but he tries hard and with considerably more experience would make an average officer.'

Pearce Harvey's superior, Group Captain Norman Odbert, another regular, and former commanding officer of 64 Squadron during the Battle of Britain, was perhaps even less conciliatory, suggesting that John was 'a slow worker inclined to give too much time to one job at the expense of another'.

Unperturbed by his superior's view of his so far unremarkable career, John applied for, and was granted, extended service, committing Angela to life as a service wife. This was a difficult time for a couple with young children living a peripatetic existence, not quite settling in one location before being obliged to up-sticks and move to another. The situation was to become even more difficult when in the summer of 1947 he received an overseas posting, returning to the Middle East and the scene of his first tour, five years earlier.

The Canal Zone in Egypt had changed little since his last visit, though the enemy had changed. Palestine had erupted into civil war leading to the creation of the state of Israel. In Egypt there were uprisings that forced the British to withdraw to the Canal Zone in 1948, and which would eventually lead to the Suez War in 1956.

In the immediate term, however, John concerned himself with his role as a supernumerary administrative officer at Headquarters Middle East before being posted to RAF Deversoir on the northwest shore of the Great Bitter Lake. What his former CO had taken for being slow, another, Squadron Leader Albert Malster, interpreted as being 'unhurried' and therefore 'apt to be misinterpreted as laziness'. Malster, a former NCO pilot who had been commissioned and transferred to the admin and special duties branch, was arguably closer to John in experience. The elderly station commander and First World War veteran Group Captain Cecil Aston similarly praised his adjutant for doing a good job in difficult circumstances, supporting the station commander with the day-to-day running of the base.

John thrived in his role and grew as an individual. Previously criticised for being slipshod, he was now applauded for his 'noteworthy attention to detail'. Sometimes viewed as being aloof and lacking in humour, Malster saw John as having 'a pleasant personality', and a man who was 'a good mixer, and is popular with his fellow officers'.

The RAF after the war was a very different service than it had been during hostilities. A great many of its number were conscripted men and all they wanted to do was leave. In my first two or three postings as adjutant or assistant adjutant, my whole life seemed to be taken up with Courts Martial for airmen who had gone absent without leave (AWOL), sometimes for weeks on end, or with Courts of Enquiry when a vehicle had been in an accident. There were huge volumes of paperwork – a Court Martial for example, required no fewer than six copies of all documents, each one having to be signed in red ink.

There was also the issue of 'station committees'. With a new labour Prime Minister, Attlee, we had to create 'committees' with representatives from every part of the station as well as the station commander, the adjutant, and the station warrant officer. We had to listen to the men's grievances and demonstrate what actions we were taking to make life better. It was little short of

*chaos. Some of the station commanders appeared not to know
what was going on outside their office door.*

*The officers who had been schooled in administration, and spent
most of their career in the Accountant Branch for example, were
the best. They were 'proper' regular officers, men like Group
Captain Aston. Others who had been flying men and pressed into
an administrative role were not so good, and although I always
felt that I got on with them well personally, they were often
dismissive of the large amounts of work we had to do.*

In all, John spent almost three years in Egypt, accompanied by his
wife and two daughters, Angela and Karen. (Karen had been born
on 30 May, 1945.) A third daughter, Maureen, was born while they
were overseas. His postings included a spell at 128 Maintenance Unit
(128 MU) and at a Base Ammunition Depot in Abu Sultan, part of a
'lodger' unit within an army camp:

*This was an army depot where ammunition and shells were
stored. We were a lodger unit there and the main challenge was
one of security. The perimeter of the base stretched for miles and
it was virtually impossible to patrol it all. It consisted of two
fences of barbed wire with a gap of about 30ft in between.*

*On one particular day, a consignment of ammunition arrived
by train. We had heard on the grapevine that a robbery was
planned for the following night; the plan was to send dogs across
the gap in the wire and then they would follow from behind. So
we set up an ambush. They came at around one in the morning,
and we watched and waited until they were on top of the trucks
and then we let them have it. Two were killed, two more wounded
and three of them got away.*

The final confidential report confirmed how John had developed into a most efficient administrative officer, though recommended that further training was required. As it was, John's time in the RAF was fast drawing to a close. Returning to the UK in February 1950, after a short period of leave, he was posted to No.1 School of Recruit Training and Technical College at Henlow before resigning his commission in September.

For the first time in more than ten years he was out of uniform.

*   *   *

John started at Smart & Browns as a stock controller before moving to the Biggleswade-based engineering giant Weatherley Oilgear in 1956 where he worked for almost twenty years. Weatherley Oilgear described itself as a company that 'made machines to produce machines' and at one time had more than 1,000 staff, making it by far and away the town's largest employer. It was subsequently taken over by Cincinnati Milocron, and when the firm began to struggle in the early 1970s, John took voluntary redundancy.

He joined British Aerospace in Stevenage as a design office librarian, responsible for managing and updating more than a quarter of a million records, before finally retiring in 1986.

Since the war, John has not shown any particular interest in reunions, though he has been an active member of the local Royal Air Force Association (RAFA) and Bomber Command Association (BCA).

In 2010 he was invited to take part in 'Exercise Halifax Shadow', an event organised by Tony Hibberd to celebrate the role of 78 Squadron during and since the Second World War. It included a gathering of no fewer than five squadron DFCs, joined by Larry Taylor, George Duffee, Freddie Johnson and Flight Lieutenant Michelle Goodman. Goodman was the first female officer to win the gallantry award as a helicopter pilot in Iraq. He hoped he might meet up with former members of his crew but it was not to be. There are today very few surviving wartime members of 78 Squadron and even fewer from his days with 148 Squadron in the desert. He is similarly one of the oldest and last, if not the very last, surviving members of the wartime Goldfish Club.

Today he lives quietly in his home in Biggleswade. He has a few momentoes from his time in the RAF: a print of a Halifax III; his goolie chit; and a handful of black and white photos including one larking about with his pals in the desert and another of 'Smithy', his second-tour skipper. He also still has his original Goldfish Club membership card, signed by the Hon. Secretary Charles Robertson. For some reason John cannot explain, the date of his qualification is wrong. It states 3 March 1941 rather than 3 March 1942.

His four daughters – Angela, Karen, Maureen and Norma – live close by and are regular visitors along with the children and grandchildren:

Like many of my age, I feel lucky to have survived when so many didn't. From a very early age I had looked after myself and have a strong sense of self-preservation. This helped sustain me through the difficult times. Somehow, if it does not sound too perverse, I miss the war. I miss the comradeship it gave you, being part of a crew, and I miss the dangers of flying. I never thought they would get me and they didn't. Others were more fatalistic; some seemed to know that they'd never make it but it wasn't like that for me. Self-discipline and determination got me through, and in an increasingly difficult and competitive world, these qualities are needed now more than ever.

As a good Catholic, born, baptised and confirmed I always had faith and God was on my side. Of course there were some upsets along the way, but generally everything has gone right. My only regret is that I still haven't won the pools.

Appendix I

Dramatis Personae – Officers and Men

At 15 OTU Harwell:

Pilot Officer Craig. Pilot William Craig was awarded a DFC for a first tour with 148 Squadron in December 1942 and a Bar with 462 Squadron the following year as a deputy flight commander. The citation for the Bar mentioned his 'undiminished ardour for operational work'. He was also later Mentioned in a Despatch. He survived the war and retired from the RAF in 1953.

Pilot Officer Hodges. Pilot Ronald Hodges followed John to 148 Squadron and flew as second pilot to Donald Crossley before taking over as captain of his own aircraft. Awarded the DFC at the end of his first tour, he returned to the UK and was Mentioned in a Despatch and subsequently awarded the Air Force Cross as an acting squadron leader.

Pilot Officer Mahood – Observer John Mahood survived the war having completed more than 100 operations, many as a navigator with 109 Squadron in 1944-45 flying Mosquitoes. He was awarded the DFC (March 1945) and DSO (October 1945 as acting squadron leader).

Sergeant R E Ralph – Wireless Operator. Robert Ralph was killed on the night of 14 January, 1945 while serving with 223 Squadron, a Bomber Support Squadron within 100 Group. He was 24.

Sergeant Brennan– Wireless Operator and Air Gunner (front gunner).

Sergeant R Van-Walwyk – Rear gunner. 35-year-old Reginald Van-Walwyk was awarded the DFM for his service with 40 Squadron in October 1942. He was subsequently killed on his second tour of operations with 100 Squadron on the night of 17 December 1943. He had been commissioned.

At 148 Squadron Kabrit:
Officers and aircrew during John's first tour of operations with 148 Squadron and their subsequent fates (where known):

Commanding Officers:

Wing Commander Frederick 'Turkey' Rainsford – Born in 1909 in Castlebar, County Mayo, (where his father was stationed as a member of the Royal Irish Constabulary), Rainsford was educated in Belfast. Rejected by the Royal Navy, he emigrated to Kenya as a pupil farmer, but returned to Belfast following the Depression to enrol at Queen's University to study agriculture. Learning to fly, he was commissioned into the RAF in 1936 and began life instructing before being posted to North Africa and taking command of 148 Squadron. Although exhausted by his experience in the desert, he recovered to take command of 115 Squadron flying Lancasters and was awarded the DFC. Surviving the war, he played a key role in the Berlin Airlift for which he was recognised with the CBE. He died in 1999.

Wing Commander John Rollinson – Born in 1912, John Dudley Robinson was a pre-war Auxiliary Air Force officer attached to 614 (County of Glamorgan) Squadron. As an acting wing commander he was awarded the DFC while flying with 38 Squadron before being posted to command 148 Squadron soon after. He was later killed in action as Officer Commanding 630 Squadron on 29 January 1944, having flown no fewer than fifty-five operations. He was 32 and left a widow, Jean.

Wing Commander James Warne – Born in 1916 in St Austell, Cornwall, Warne was granted a short service commission in the RAF at the start of 1938. At the outbreak of war he was flying Whitleys with 102 Squadron in 4 Group, being awarded the DFC in October as an acting flight lieutenant, and adding a Bar for service with 58 Squadron the following year. In the western desert, he was awarded the DSO for his command of 148 Squadron and later mentioned in despatches for distinguished service in South East Asia. He retired as a group captain CBE, DSO, DFC and died in 1991 in Surrey. His brother, Peter Ellis Warne, died on active service, killed in 1940 while serving with 107 Squadron on operations to Stavanger. He had two other brothers who served in the Army and Navy.

Flight Commanders/Senior officers:

Flight Lieutenant Baird – The Honourable Robert Baird was an Old Etonian who had originally passed out from the Royal Military Academy Sandhurst as a second lieutenant, joining the Gordon Highlanders. The son of the former Governor General of Australia, Viscount Stonehaven, Baird was posted to India and was for a time the aide-de-camp to the Viceroy, Lord Willingdon. Surprisingly unsuited to the pomp and ceremony of army life, he resigned his commission and had a brief flirtation with Hollywood in the US before returning to the UK and joining the RAF. Like many of his peers he became an instructor, and was sent to South Africa to train new pilots as part of the Empire Air Training Scheme. Posted to Egypt, he joined 70 and then 148 Squadrons, flying more than thirty operations to complete his first tour. Returning to the UK, he was later posted to 10 Squadron before rejoining his former squadron commander, 'Turkey' Rainsford, at 115 Squadron. He was killed in action on 13 July, 1943 at the age of 33, by which time his logbook had more than 2,214 flying hours recorded on aircraft ranging from a Hornet Moth to a Halifax.

Flight Lieutenant Douglas Cracknell – Born in 1909, Douglas Aubrey Cracknell had learned to fly privately with the South Coast Flying Club in Shoreham in 1935. Already an experienced flyer and instructor upon the outbreak of war, his tour with 148 Squadron was followed by a return to the UK and a further tour with 49 Squadron for which he was awarded the DFC. Joining the elite Pathfinder Force, Cracknell was awarded the DSO in November 1944 with 35 Squadron on his third tour, and added a Bar to his DFC as Officer Commanding 7 Squadron, his citation crediting him with seventy-five operations, 18 as Master Bomber. After the war he became chief pilot for British South American Airways. At the time of his death in 1979, Cracknell had logged nearly 6,000 flying hours and flown well over one million miles.

Flight Lieutenant Thomas Prickett – Born in Lindfield, Sussex, and educated at Haileybury, Thomas Prickett spent five years in India with Begg Sutherland, the sugar business, and served as a trooper with the Bihar Light Horse. Joining the RAF in 1937, Prickett spent the first three years of service as a flying instructor both in England and Southern Rhodesia. Anxious to fly operations, he was posted to 148 Squadron in 1941, flying his thirty-second and final operation of his first tour in July 1942, after which he was awarded the DFC. After time in the US, again as an instructor, he returned for a second tour, this time as a flight commander with 103 Squadron in the spring of 1943. On completion of another thirty operations he was awarded the DSO. After the war he attained high rank, playing a prominent role in the planning of the ill-fated Suez operation of 1956. He retired as an air chief marshal and died in 2010.

Squadron Leader Arthur Craigie – Craigie was awarded the DFC in February 1943, his citation making mention of several determined attacks on *Tobruk*. On one occasion, after setting course for base, he returned to the target area and dived to 3,000ft to release a large bomb, which had not released in his first attack, on a heavy gun position. On another he descended to 700ft to rake a column of tanks and vehicles with machine gun fire. A large fire was started and much confusion ensued. On another flight he disorganised a convoy of motor transport by his bombing. The citation read: 'Squadron Leader Craigie has invariably displayed skill and courage of a high order. His untiring efforts and inspiring example have been reflected in the fine fighting qualities of his squadron'. He was later killed in July 1943 when his aircraft was obliged to ditch with engine trouble and the Wellington broke its back. Only one of his crew – the navigator – survived.

Flight Lieutenant Tony Hayter – Tony Hayter joined the RAF on a Short Service Commission and was posted to 57 Squadron at Montdidier, just as the Phoney War became real. He flew his first reconnaissance of the German/Dutch border on 10 May. It was almost his last. Intercepted by no fewer than three Bf109s, he only just managed to evade their attentions to land at Villeneuve with more than 200 bullet holes in his machine. Two weeks later he was mentioned in despatches for flying a British army officer to Merryville to impart plans for the evacuation of Dunkirk. Back in the UK, Tony converted to Wellingtons and in March 1941 began bomber operations over Northern Europe. After only a month he was posted to the Middle East, stopping over in Malta before progressing to Egypt as part of 253 Communications Flight, transporting men and spare parts between the various landing grounds dotted around the western desert. Keen to return to the bombing war, he was posted to 148 Squadron in January 1942 and lost on 24 April. Ultimately incarcerated in Stalag Luft III, he was one of 'The Fifty' shot in The Great Escape.

At 78 Squadron Breighton:

Wing Commander Duncan Hyland Smith – born in November 1918, Hyland Smith joined the RAF in 1938 and spent much of the early part of his flying career as an instructor. He completed a tour of operations with 78 Squadron as a flight commander before being posted to 102 Squadron as Officer Commanding for the last few weeks of the war. He was granted a permanent commission in 1946 and enjoyed a full peacetime career, including a spell as Officer Commanding The Queen's Flight in the 1950s for which he was admitted as a Member of the Victorian Order. He retired as Air Commodore D.F. Hyland Smith CBE, MVO, DFC, AFC and died on 21 December 1987.

Appendix II

Gallantry Awards – 1942–43

Distinguished Service Order:
Wing Commander James Warne DFC   22.1.43

Bar to Distinguished Flying Cross:
Flight Lieutenant Alwyn Hamman   7.4.42   Killed in action 31.5.42

Distinguished Flying Cross

Flight Lieutenant Robert Alexander	7.4.42	RCAF Observer – 51 ops
Flying Officer Neville Cowan	7.4.42	Mentioned in despatches 1954
Flying Officer Alec Cranswick	7.4.42	KIA 5.7.44
Warrant Officer John Grehan	15.5.42	Retired 1961
Flight Lieutenant Robert Church	2.6.42	RCAF. Observer – 41 ops
Flying Officer Richard Milburn	2.6.42	MiD
Pilot Officer Donald Crossley	2.6.42	KIA 24.11.43
Flight Lieutenant Alfred Woodley	18.9.42	
Pilot Officer Alan Hardy	18.9.42	RAAF
Squadron Leader Thomas Prickett	6.10.42	DSO Later Air Chief Marshal
Flying Officer Lancelot Baron	6.10.42	
Flying Officer Ronald Hodges	6.10.42	AFC MiD
Flying Officer William Craig	4.12.42	
Flying Officer Jeffrey Pelletier	4.12.42	RAAF. Bar to DFC
Pilot Officer Albert Loos	22.1.43	
Flying Officer Ian Lawson	30.1.43	Bar to DFC. Later Air Vice Marshal
Flying Officer Wallace Watson	30.1.43	
Pilot Officer Fred Watson	5.2.43	

Distinguished Flying Medals:

Sergeant Francis Adams	7.4.42	Later commissioned
Sergeant John Robinson	7.4.42	
Sergeant Alfred Sudden	7.4.42	KIA 6.7.44 as Squadron Leader
Flight Sergeant Stephen Geary	15.5.42	KIA 2.5.44 as Flight Lieutenant
Flight Sergeant Christopher Chalmers	15.5.42	Later commissioned. DFC
Flight Sergeant Stanley Lee	2.6.42	Later commissioned. AFC
Sergeant Allan Brisbane	2.6.42	Later commissioned
Sergeant Alexander Hutchinson	7.7.42	Later commissioned
Flight Sergeant Bruce McNab	6.10.42	RCAF
Sergeant Kenneth Elcoate	6.10.42	Later commissioned
Sergeant George Barton	4.12.42	Later commissioned
Flight Sergeant James McDonald	22.1.43	RAAF. KIA 13.8.44
Sergeant Douglas Chinery	22.1.43	Later commissioned
Sergeant Charles Klimcke	5.2.43	Later Captain of BEA Comet Flight
Sergeant Donald Moon	5.2.43	Killed in training. 5.9.43
Sergeant Herbert Tricks	5.2.43	Killed in training. 14.1.45

Notes

Chapter 1

1. The twin-engined Dornier 217 was a larger version of the better known Dornier 17 'Flying Pencil' so called because of its narrow fuselage. Initially designed as a medium bomber, later in the war the Do 217 was pressed into service as a nightfighter.
2. The Lewis Gun had been designed in the UK in 1911 and used extensively by British Forces throughout the First World War. It had a rate of fire of up to 600 rounds per minute, and an effective range of around 900yds. Its distinctive tubular barrel was complemented by a similarly distinct magazine 'drum' (or 'pan') that held either forty-seven or ninety-seven rounds. As an airborne weapon, the Lewis was superseded by the Vickers K – a machine gun with almost twice the rate of fire.
3. Joe (Joseph Edmund Brookes) was shot down in the Middle East and broke both his legs. Making a full recovery, Joe later flew with 10 Squadron, completing his second tour. In May 1945 he joined John at Westcott near Aylesbury dealing with former POWs.
4. Boore was awarded his DFM in May 1940 as a flight sergeant with 115 Squadron. He survived the war to retire as a squadron leader in 1960. Wilde had been awarded his DFM in the summer of 1940 flying with 38 Squadron.
5. Maitland had been a naval cadet and transferred to the Royal Naval Air Service (RNAS) at the start of the First World War to become an airship pilot. He survived a crash in the Firth of Forth and after the cessation of hostilities was granted a permanent commission in the RAF. By the outbreak of the Second World War he was a group captain. He later went on to senior command as AOC 93 (OTU) Group and retired as Air Vice Marshal in 1950. He died in 1985.
6. The 10 Captains of aircraft were Wing Commander J. H. T. Simpson, Pilot Officer William Craig, Flight Sergeants Frederick Ellison and Harold Vertican, and Sergeants Lomas, More, Hammett, Knowles, Webb and Wheal. Edward Lomas went on to win the DFM and earn a commission. Frederick Ellison retired in 1957 as Squadron Leader Frederick Ellison

OBE, AFC. Jack Webb was commissioned and awarded the DFC at the end of the war for services with 544 Squadron, a photographic reconnaissance unit (PRU).
7. During October 1941, 29 of the 31 aircraft arrived, one having taken a direct flight across France to Malta!

Chapter 2
1. Their aircraft was a Wellington II, Z8352. The Wellington II was similar in all other ways to the Wellington 1C, the most numerous of all variants, other than the engines. The Wellington II was powered by 1145hp Rolls Royce Merlin X engines in preference to the Bristol Pegasus.
2. The official report differs slightly from John's own recollection, suggesting that the pilot attempted to land with one wing low and lost an engine (possibly starved of fuel). He swerved to avoid another aircraft, a tyre burst and the undercarriage collapsed. Either way, the aircraft was never repaired and eventually destroyed in an air raid a few months later.

Chapter 3
1. Kellett was shortly after posted to the Long Range Development Unit at Upper Heyford as a flight commander. He was later the Senior Air Staff Officer with 205 Group before being shot down and becoming the Senior British Officer (SBO) within Stalag Luft III.
2. Because John's log book was stolen in the 1950s, it is difficult to determine the exact date of his arrival at Kabrit. There is an entry in the operations record book (ORB) for 22 November that reads: 'one sergeant w/op AG arrived on posting'. This is the only mention of a single w/op AG being posted in that month.
3. Baird and Rainsford were close personal friends, Rainsford describing Baird as a 'wild, lovely, irrepressible Scotsman'. When Rainsford later took command of 115 Squadron, Baird joined him as one of his Flight Commanders. He was later killed in action.
4. Halazone was a chlorine-based water purification tablet.
5. The 4,000lb high capacity bomb, referred to commonly as the 'blockbuster' was the first of the large blast bombs to be designed for use by the Royal Air Force. Of cast steel construction and measuring more than nine ft in length, the requirements for such a bomb had been laid down by the Air Ministry in September 1940, one of the criteria being that it could be carried by the Wellington bomber. It is interesting to note that a Wellington carrying a single 4,000lb HC carried more than two-and-a-half times the actual amount

of explosive than it did when armed with its 'usual' eighteen 250lb or nine 500lb general purpose (GP) bombs. The bombs were formally introduced into service in January 1942, though they were certainly being used by 148 Squadron in November and December 1941. Over 93,000 blockbusters had been dropped by the end of the war with devastating effect.

6. 70 Squadron penned the following, to be sung to the tune of Clementine: 'Seventy Squadron, Seventy Squadron, though we say it with a sigh, we must do the ruddy mail run every night until we die'. Sadly many of them did.

7. Derek Skinner had the unusual middle name of Lahee. He had won the DFC with 44 Squadron, promulgated in May 1941.

8. Cracknell ended the war as a wing commander with the DSO, DFC & Bar for operations with 49 Squadron, and 35 and 7 Squadrons of Pathfinder Force. He completed three tours.

9. Baird's log book entry reads: Operations (18). Target enemy transport at Buerat El Hsun (west of Sirte). Load thirteen 250lbs and incendiaries. Target located and bombed. Pilot Officer Geary shot down by flak ship in flames.

10. Abbott was one of the Squadron's South African pilots who had joined the RAF on a short service commission in 1937. His DFC had been gazetted in November 1941 for gallantry and devotion to duty in the execution of air operations. A report on interrogations of local residents after the war and investigations carried out in Elevsis and Salamis areas state that an aircraft was shot down and crashed into the sea two miles south of Elevsis on 19 January 1942. It also stated that the Germans made a search of the area and could find no trace of the aircraft or crew. Elevsis is on the coast approx ten miles North West of Athens, whilst Salamis is six miles south west of Elevsis on the island of Kuluri. It was assumed that the aircraft crashed in the sea near Elevsis and that the crew were drowned.

11. Mackie had joined 148 from 15 Squadron at Wyton. On his return to the UK he took part in the first 1,000 bomber raid before being posted to 115 Squadron. He flew more than seventy operations over Germany and occupied France, being awarded the DSO and DFC before the war's end. After the war he became a Liberal MP and died in February 2015 as Lord Mackie of Benshie.

12. Perhaps the AOC had some empathy with the men. Earlier in his career, while Officer Commanding Northolt, he had disagreed violently with his superior's actions and the Air Ministry plans for the development of a new monoplane fighter, which resulted in him being placed under close arrest!

13. Group Captain Joseph Stewart Temple Fall DSC & Two Bars, AFC was a thirty-six-victory ace of the First World War. He retired in 1945 and died in 1988.

14. Wells was lost in a tragic accident in March 1942 returning from Egypt, when his aircraft crashed in atrocious weather conditions in high ground in Eire. Nearly all of the Liberator's crew and passengers were killed. In the 108 Squadron ORB it simply states: Wing Commander R. J. Wells DFC, by his splendid leadership, enthusiasm and zest for operations built up for this Squadron a worthy reputation. It was his ambition to have the Squadron re-equipped with Liberators and it was with this end view that he proceeded to the UK. All who knew him were impressed by his remarkable courage, his sense of justice and his interest in the welfare of all ranks. His personality and high spirits made him a favourite with all – his loss is deeply felt.

15. Flight Lieutenant Alfred Cuthbert Woodley had arrived on the squadron at the end of January. He was awarded the DFC in September 1942. He survived the war.

16. Baird reported a total eclipse of the moon!

17. The Sea Rescue Flight was established in August 1941. Initially based at Kabrit, it operated from a variety of airfields as far west as Benghazi, such was the fluidity of the front line at the time. It had both Wellington and Blenheim aircraft for search duties, although any of the local squadrons could also be involved in the search, especially if it was one of their own crews that was missing. It was not until November 1941 that the Flight acquired its first seaplanes, when the first of several ex-Fleet Air Arm Walruses began to arrive. It also acquired, uniquely, a single-engined Fairchild 91 and a twin-engined Grumman Goose, both of which had been purchased second-hand by a New York-based charity and donated to the RAF. These amphibious aircraft picked up more than twenty men during 1942 alone.

Chapter 4

1. Donald Moon, a married man, completed a tour of operations with 148 and was awarded the DFM at the start of 1943. He returned to the UK as an instructor at 20 OTU at RAF Elgin in Scotland. Moon was killed in September 1943 when an engine cut shortly after take-off and the aircraft, a Wellington X, dived straight in, killing all on board.

2. By the end of 1942 the Late Arrivals Club had 345 members.

3. Both aircraft were passed to 104.

4. Wellingtons were equipped with a 1.5lb incendiary device to be used to destroy the aircraft if brought down over enemy territory.

5. Lieutenant Colonel A.C. Thomas MC. Dodds was captured and made prisoner of war. One other member of the crew, the second pilot, also made it home.
6. The Martin Baltimore was a development of the Martin Maryland, both types being originally designed as an attack bomber. The Westland Lysander was a high-wing monoplane used as an army co-operation aircraft.
7. *Royal Air Force 1939–1945: Volume II – The Flight Avails* by Denis Richards and Hilary St. George Saunders.
8. His second pilot that night was 18-year-old Sergeant Philip Plum.
9. Ross was awarded the DFC in February 1943. He was later shot down with 428 Squadron on 13 July 1943 over Aachen.
10. Sergeant T.B.Henry RNZAF. Chandler is listed as an observer in his funeral records.

Chapter 5
1. 91 Group was headquartered in Abingdon.
2. David Ivor Phorson MacNair. MacNair was an Old Cranwellian, having been granted a permanent commission in the summer of 1931. Among his contemporaries was Wilf Oulton, an accomplished Coastal Command pilot who rose to become Air Vice-Marshal and win the DSO and DFC 'double'. MacNair was later promoted to group captain and was awarded the OBE in the New Year's Honours of 1956.
3. Possibly David Alexander Dunlop, who later flew with 7 Squadron.
4. Joe was shot down on the night of 25 June 1942 during an attack on enemy forces in and around Sidi Barrani. His Wellington was attacked by a Junkers 88 and set on fire. Joe escaped along with the wireless operator. Both were in fact rescued by a contingent of the 7th Armoured Division. The rest of the crew, including the 21-year-old pilot Paul Street, were all killed.
5. The AOC of 91 Group who interviewed John was Air Commodore Hugh Walmsley OBE, MC, DFC. Walmsley, a former pilot and flight commander within the Royal Flying Corps, was a regular visitor to the station. He was replaced by Air Vice Marshal John Gray who had first served in the Royal Naval Air Service (RNAS) before transferring to the RAF in April 1918 and becoming a flight commander with 211 Squadron. In 1941 he had been awarded the George Medal for entering a burning aircraft to save the crew.
6. His appointment appeared in the London Gazette on 16 June.
7. 1658 HCU lost seventy-two aircraft during its time at Riccall.

Chapter 6

1. Whether this story is true or not is an interesting debate. While the VC was typically and almost exclusively for one-off acts of heroism, the award of a VC to the famous bomber pilot Leonard Cheshire for a sustained period of heroism set a precedent that could have led to similar recognition for Tait.
2. Wing Commander John Ninnem Young formally took command of the Squadron the week ending 13 September. Markland received the DSO for his leadership.
3. Another 78 Squadron pilot, Ken 'Shorty' Long, witnessed the same incident. He saw one of the aircraft pull its nose up and collide with the belly of the other. He also reported that his rear gunner spotted one parachute as the aircraft fell away. Long describes the incident as occurring during the attack on Dijon in August, but no crews were lost in this raid. It is likely that the incident to which he refers is this one.
4. Crews in their post raid briefing were always asked if they had suffered any hang ups. It was not unknown for a returning crew to only casually mention that a 'Cookie' was still in their bomb bay and had not told the Armaments Officer! At this point, panic usually ensued to make the bomb 'safe'.
5. Wanganui was the code word given to a blind pathfinding technique that comprised sky marking, and was used when a target was obscured by cloud. Pathfinders would mark a point in the sky at which the main force should aim its bombs and (hopefully) hit the target.

Chapter 7

1. The flight engineer was Sergeant William Bailey. The citation that appeared in the London Gazette on 22 September read: 'One night in July, 1944, this officer and airman were captain and flight engineer respectively of an aircraft detailed to attack a target in North France. After the target had been bombed, the bomber was attacked by an enemy fighter and sustained severe damage. A fire broke out within the aircraft and an explosion occurred in Sergeant Bailey's compartment wounding him in both legs. Disregarding his injuries, this airman fought the fire until the flames were quelled. Meanwhile Flying Officer Buchanan, who had been severely burnt about the face, flew the aircraft on a level course. This officer and airman have completed many sorties and have at all times displayed courage, fortitude and determination of a high order'. Bailey was not flying on the night his skipper was lost, his place being taken by Sergeant R J Baron.
2. 'Dickey' Bird had learned to speak Russian before the war and accompanied Sir Stafford Cripps on his Mission to Moscow in 1941 as Deputy to the Senior Air Commander, Air Vice Marshal Conrad Collier, who had himself

fought in Russia in 1919. After the war he returned to Moscow in 1951 as Air Attaché and died in suspicious circumstances following a dinner to celebrate the investiture for the new UK ambassador.

3. Hubbard completed a tour of operations and was awarded the DFC. After the war he went on to become a notable test pilot, testing and evaluating the latest fast jets. Among the more unusual aircraft he flew was the so-called 'flying bedstead', an early experimental airframe which paved the way for the development of the Harrier.

4. The German nightfighter strength increased from 800 aircraft in July 1944 to 1,020 aircraft in October 1944. The total numbers engaged against RAF Bomber Command increased from 685 to 830 in the same period.

5. North Pickenham, near Swaffham, was home to the 491st Bomb Group.

Sources and Further Reading

As much of this book is as original as possible from the memories of John Brennan and associated research. Principal sources include:

RAF Officers Record of Service for John Michael Brennan – various years

AIR2/8748   Gallantry award lists and citations
AIR28/107   RAF Station Breighton ORB
AIR28/108   RAF Station Breighton ORB (appendices)
AIR29/659   15 Operational Training Unit
AIR29/661   15 Operational Training Unit (appendices)
AIR29/662   19 Operational Training Unit
AIR29/663   19 Operational Training Unit (photographs)

ORB 148 Squadron
ORB 70 Squadron
ORB 78 Squadron

The log book of Squadron Leader The Honourable Robert Baird
RAF Middle East – the official story of air operations February 1942 – January
    1943. HMSO
The Rise and Fall of the German Air Force – Air Ministry Pamphlet No 248 –
    1948

The following books were also consulted and/or are suggested for further reading:

Aircraft of the Royal Air Force Since 1918 (Putnam seventh edition, 1979) – Owen
    Thetford
Bomber Command Losses Vols 1–8 (Midland Counties) Bill Chorley
Bomber Losses in the Middle East & Mediterranean Vol 1 (Midland Counties) –
    David Gunby & Pelham Temple

Bombers Over Sand and Snow (Pen & Sword, 2011) Alun Granfield
In for a Penny, in for a Pound (Stoddart Publishing, 2000) – Howard Hewer
The Battle of Malta (William Kimber, 1980) – Joseph Attard
Wellington Wings (William Kimber, 1980) – F. Roy Chappell